T4-AFY-158

HERBART

The Great Educators

EDITED BY NICHOLAS MURRAY BUTLER

HERBART

AND THE HERBARTIANS

BY

CHARLES DE GARMO, PH.D.

PRESIDENT OF SWARTHMORE COLLEGE, PENNSYLVANIA

GEN. THEO. SEMINARY
LIBRARY
NEW YORK

NEW YORK
CHARLES SCRIBNER'S SONS
1912

92
H 4139

66601

COPYRIGHT, 1895, BY

CHARLES SCRIBNER'S SONS.

GEN. THEO. SEMINARY
LIBRARY
NEW YORK

F 24 '20

PREFACE

THE purpose of this volume is to give a bird's-eye view of Herbart and his doctrines of education, both as presented by himself, and as developed by his successors. In English-speaking countries his system of educational thought is for most teachers still in the stage of exposition; furthermore, the beginner in every well-organized, far-reaching system is always in need of an introduction. To the teacher, therefore, who inquires for the leading purposes of this school, and the methods whereby it is sought to realize them, this book attempts an intelligible answer. It concerns itself but little with Herbart's metaphysics, and rigorously refrains from introducing confusing refinements of doctrine. It confines its attention strictly to essentials. Only epoch-making men and their chief contributions are considered at all. If, therefore, among so many men worthy of mention, so few are treated, and even with these the discussion confined to essentials, the reason must be sought in the purpose to make clear to the inquiring teacher what the Herbartians are trying to do and how they are trying to do it.

The ultimate purpose of the Herbartians may be said to be the development of character, not in a nar-

row subjective sense, but in a broad social one. They
seek to fit the child for every important phase of
family, social, civil, religious, and economic life, — to
develop, in short, the whole boy or girl. In this broad
aim they are, perhaps, not peculiar; but they have
certainly made some contributions as to the means for
accomplishing this end, so devoutly to be desired for
public education. The strength of their position is,
that they show how under favorable circumstances
this result can be achieved with the agencies already
at the command of the school; namely, the common-
school studies as they may be taught, together with
the ordinary discipline of the school. They believe
that, properly selected, articulated, and taught, the
common branches of an elementary education are
potent influences in training the child's moral insight
and disposition.

But this training must be in full harmony with the
nature of the child's mind, and especially with his
moral and intellectual apperception, or assimilative
power. We find, consequently, that the burning
questions with this body of teachers pertain, first, to
the selection and sifting of suitable subject-matter
in the various studies; then to its rational articulation or coördination; and finally, to the truest and
best methods of teaching it to the child. Every
teacher will recognize that this purpose and these
means are the important things in education.

                                    CHARLES De GARMO.

SWARTHMORE COLLEGE,
      October, 1894.

CONTENTS

PART III

HERBARTIAN IDEAS IN AMERICA

CHAPTER I

CHAPTER II

CHAPTER III

CHAPTER IV

Part I

HERBART'S CONTRIBUTION TO EDUCATION

HERBART AND THE HERBAR-TIANS

CHAPTER I

WHAT PESTALOZZI LEFT FOR HERBART TO DO

WHAT the labors of Pestalozzi have done for German education were long to tell. It concerns us more for present purposes to know what he left undone. The world has read the history of Germany's brilliant educational development, whose initial stages are found in the work of the Swiss Reformer, his disciples and successors. The story need not be retold. The schools of the United States, so far as educational theory is concerned, trace their origin in large part to the same primal sources. But because these men did so much, it does not follow that they did everything. Like all great reforms, that begun by Pestalozzi was emotional rather than scientific in its initial stages. Exact and logical thought does not stir a nation into a great movement for the educational uplifting of the masses, but serves rather to give direction and efficiency to what has been set in motion by moral forces. Pestalozzi was a true reformer. He could see the end to be reached, he could rouse all Europe to the sore need of the people, he could expose the barrenness of formal teaching, he could announce universal principles; but in directing his pupils over the long road that leads from ignorance to knowledge, from untutored natural disposition to moral freedom, he could indeed rely upon the guidance that comes of faith, but not so surely upon that which comes from sight. This for him was doubtless best, but for the generations of teachers to follow, who could not be fired with his divine enthusiasm, it became as necessary to see as to believe.

For a very good reason, however, Pestalozzi is excusable for not establishing his instruction upon a firm psychological basis. At that time, no psychology in the modern sense of the term existed. It is true that Immanuel Kant had developed his system of the rational presuppositions that make mind and experience possible, but he had studiously neglected experience itself, so that his work had little or no effect in determining how the mind of the child shall be trained. The current psychology of the day was, for the most part, that of Aristotle plus a good many misconceptions that had gradually accumulated in the common mind. This, added to the fact that Pestalozzi's reform had its sources in the heart rather than in the head, enables us to understand that there was something left for Herbart to do; namely, to give scientific precision to instruction and moral training by founding them upon an adequate system of psychology and ethics.

Bacon describes three classes of thinkers, comparing them to three insects, the spider, the ant, and the bee. Some men, like the spider, he says, spin all their knowledge out of themselves; some collect it indiscriminately like the ant; while others gather facts wherever they can find them, and from these facts bring forth new products by means of their own thoughtful elaboration, just as the bee produces honey from the sweets he has gathered from the flowers. Pestalozzi's method of investigation seems to have been the kind mentioned first. He looked into his own heart and mind for the laws of mental growth, formulated them, and forthwith began to spin his theories of instruction. Thus, in one place he says: "In these laws I believe I shall certainly find the threads out of which a universal psychological method of instruction can be spun. Man! say I to myself, in dreamy search for these threads, in the ripening of every species of fruit, you recognize in all its parts the result of the wholly perfected product, and you must regard no human judgment as ripe that does not appear in all its parts as the result of complete observation of the object considered."

The following are examples of these general principles of instruction, empirically received, from which Pestalozzi seeks to evolve the methods of teaching: —

1. "Learn, therefore, to arrange thy perceptions, and to complete the simple before proceeding to the complex.

2. "Further, bring together in thy mind all those things which essentially belong together, in the same connection in which they are actually found in nature.

3. "Strengthen and intensify thy impression of important objects by bringing them nearer through art, and by making them act upon thee through the different senses.

4. "Regard all the effects of physical nature as absolutely necessary, and recognize in this necessity the result of the power with which they unify their apparently heterogeneous elements to the realization of their purpose; and let the art with which thou, through instruction, workest upon thy race, as well as the results which it effects, be elevated to a like physical necessity, so that in all of thy doing, all means, however heterogeneous in appearance, work together for the accomplishment of their great purpose.

5. "But richness and variety in environment and excitation cause the results of physical necessity to bear the impress of freedom and independence."

"From these individual principles," he again remarks, "we may spin out the threads of a universal and psychological method of instruction."

Like an impetuous leader with an army before a river, Pestalozzi does not wait to build a bridge, but bids all rush in. Many get over; yet some are lost, and all are wet.

Looking at the query, What was left for Herbart to do? from another standpoint, we shall see that one of the main results of the labors of Comenius, Rousseau, and Pestalozzi is the firmly fixed conviction that observation, or the use of the senses, and in general the consideration of simple concrete facts in every field of knowledge, is the sure foundation upon which all right elementary education rests. This truth is now the acknowledged starting-point of all scientific methods of teaching, yet the fact of the importance of observation in instruction does not carry with it any information showing how the knowledge so obtained can be utilized, or what its nature, time, amount, and order of presentation should be. In short, it does not show how mental assimilation can best take place, or how the resulting acquisitions can be made most efficiently to influence the emotional and volitional side of our nature. Perception is, indeed, the first stage in cognition, but its equally important correlative is apperception, or mental assimilation. It is Herbart and his successors who have made us distinctly conscious of this fact. The following paragraph from Dr. William T. Harris confirms the view here taken: "The progress of education is in a zigzag line, from extreme to extreme. This appears throughout all history. But were it not that succeeding times profit by the experience of their forerunners, the progress would not be assured. The history of the good and bad incident to one extreme is sufficient to prevent its repetition. The extremes are new ones at least in substantial features, and not a discouraging survival of past issues. At one time the schools have tended almost exclusively to memory-culture, with very little attempt at verification by original research and observation. This was the case with what is called the old education, and if we are to believe the critics, this ought to be called the prevailing system of our time also. But Pestalozzi exploded the theory on which it rests and substituted another. He laid stress on sense-preception, verification, and original research. The practice of our time may not correspond to its theory, but certainly all writers uphold the Pestalozzian doctrine of instruction by object-lessons. But while this reform is progressing towards its extreme, another tendency has begun within a few years, and it promises to force a new departure on our zigzag line. This is the doctrine of Herbart, which holds that it is not so much sense-perception that is wanted in education as apperception — not so much seeing and hearing and handling things, as recognizing them and understanding them. The Herbartian trend on our zigzag of progress helps to reënforce sense-perception by the memory, through the use of the causal series of ideas. It therefore combines the two former trends in a higher. Doubtless there will be new trends on the zigzag of progress to correct the extremes and errors of Herbartianism, but, compared with Pestalozzi's theory of intellectual instruction, or with that other and older theory of memory as the sole intellectual faculty, there can be no doubt that the Herbartians are right." [1]

Closely allied to the fact that Herbart gave the initial impulse to this combination of memory and perception in apperception, is another of almost equal importance. "The natural harmonious development of all the powers of a human being for the sake of his true moral nature" is a principle to which Pestalozzi ever recurs. "It is," says Vogel, "the new principle of Pestalozzi's pedagogics. True, Comenius and Rousseau declared for an education in accordance with nature. But whereas Comenius by 'nature' understood the external world of plants and animals and physical forces, and Rousseau meant nature as opposed to art, Pestalozzi penetrated to the depths of

[1] Dr. William T. Harris, U. S. Commissioner of Education, *Educational Review*, May, 1893.

human nature, since he found this principle in moral feeling, in the freedom that is guided by duty." [1]

Herbart fully accepts Pestalozzi's statement of the ultimate end of education, but attempts to show how the daily activity of the school may bring about this desirable result, — a problem that Pestalozzi never solved for others. It is a cardinal doctrine with all followers of Herbart, that instruction itself should consciously work toward moral ends. The watch-word upon their banner is *Erziehender Unterricht;* that is, instruction that makes for character. It is to a scientific study of psychology and ethics in their application to teaching that they look for guidance in the matter.

Briefly summarizing, Pestalozzi, his contemporaries, and successors, left a threefold work for Herbart to do, as follows: 1. The development of a psychology capable of immediate bearing on the problems of teaching; 2. The scientific application of this psychology to education; and 3. The revelation of the possibility of making *all* the activities of the school-room, including especially instruction, bear directly upon the development of moral character.

We should not regard Herbart's contributions as additions, however important, to an educational mosaic already existing. Such a view would be most misleading. His work is fundamental, compelling a new elaboration of the whole theory of education. Whenever the world has discovered a new principle or method of thought, all its work has been done

[1] Dr. August Vogel, *Geschichte der Pädagogik als Wissenschaft*, p. 161.

over again. Bacon's revival of the inductive method
was not an addition to science, but a revolution in
science. The results wrought out in the Middle Ages
were discarded or wholly revised. Since Darwin and
his fellow-workers established the theory of evolution as a standpoint in thinking, the whole field of
knowledge has been reëxamined in accordance with
the new principle. Not only the natural sciences, but
ethics, religion, psychology, and even metaphysics,
have felt the leavening influence of the evolutionist.
It takes a large volume to record the progress of the
last ten years in bacteriology. No student of this
science regards it as a mere addition to the sum of
medical knowledge, but it is to him a new standpoint
from which to reëxamine all medical and surgical
science. The psycho-physicist does not dream of re-
stricting his investigations to the interaction between
mind and body, but claims the whole dominion of
psychology, if not of metaphysics, for the application
of his method; that is, he too must open up again in a
new way all that other methods claim to have settled.
Copernicus did not add new circles to the already complicated system of Ptolemy; he wrought out a new
astronomy with the old stars. In a similiar way, Herbart, using the same facts of human nature and experience, the same materials and means of instruction and
training, brings forth new products through the application of new principles. As Dr. Harris says, the
two old stages of education, memory and perception,
are united by him into the higher one of apperception,
or mental assimilation. The laws of mental development are examined anew; each branch of instruction

is studied in its relations to the pupil's needs, understanding, and interests, and all the studies of the curriculum are considered in their double relations to one another and to the apperception of the pupil. Finally, the truest and best methods of uniting these two factors, the mind of the child and the materials of instruction and training, are investigated.   This treatment is comparable in kind to that of the modern astronomer, bacteriologist, psycho-physicist, or evolutionist ; it is creative work.

CHAPTER II

HERBART'S LIFE AND WORKS

The times in which Herbart and Pestalozzi lived were at once the age of heroic speculative thought in the universities and the age of economic and political degradation among the common people. The heart of the reformer, Pestalozzi, responded to the one, the mind of the thinker, Herbart, to the other; for the native forces of the mind exert themselves in accordance with surrounding intellectual and moral influences. Furthermore, minds become fertilized at an early age by the spirit of the times. Lectures on philosophy were given at the gymnasium attended by the youthful Herbart, and we find him at the early age of fourteen writing essays on the moral freedom of man. At the age of eighteen, when most boys are in these days just entering upon their freshman work in college, Herbart was a diligent student of German philosophy under Fichte at Jena. To gain recognition, Fichte had introduced himself to Kant at Königsberg by means of an *Essay toward a Critique of all Revelation,* which was for a time ascribed to Kant himself. In a somewhat similar manner, Herbart

12

attracted Fichte's attention, by handing him essays concerning certain doubtful statements in the *Science of Knowledge*. During his second year at the university, he gave Fichte a critique of two of Schelling's works, in which he broke away from the ruling Idealism of the times, and laid in some measure the groundwork of his own future system of philosophy.

John Frederick Herbart was born at Oldenburg on the 4th of May, 1776. He died a professor at Göttingen in 1841. His life-span reached over the period of great political revolutions and through that of the evolution of great systems of thought. The turbulence of the times does not seem to have modified essentially his course of life. Fichte, his teacher, was caught in the grip of the age, and besides being the Idealistic philosopher became the firebrand of German patriotism; but Herbart fought only the spectres of the mind. His field of labor was the university classroom; his companions were, not armed soldiers of the camp, but spectacled students and professors of the halls of learning. While Pestalozzi was dealing with the unkempt urchins of poverty, and Froebel with the children of the kindergarten, Herbart was in the university instructing the future leaders of thought. Herbart's experience as a teacher would seem too small a thing to mention — some two or three years in a private family in Switzerland with three children aged respectively eight, twelve, and fourteen. Yet to a man who can see an oak tree in an acorn, *i.e.*, who can understand all minds from the study of a few, such an experience may be most fruitful.

At the close of his university career, Herbart, then a young man twenty-one years old, accepted an invitation to become tutor to the three older children of Herr von Steiger, Governor of Interlaken, Switzerland. The most helpful thing to him about this experience was that he was required to make a written bi-monthly report to his employer concerning the study, conduct, and progress of his charges. Five of these reports have been published; nothing is known of the others. An extended biography would doubtless warrant a careful analysis of these reports, since they are full of anticipations of the educational ideals that Herbart afterward elaborated. Yet, though "coming events cast their shadows before," a brief exposition must content itself with the essentials of Herbart's developed system, leaving the tracing of these anticipations to those who have time and inclination for the task.

After resigning his tutorship in Switzerland, Herbart went to Bremen to prepare himself for an academic career in the university. He stopped at Jena for a time, and then visited his parents at Oldenburg, to whom he showed his consideration by offering to yield his preferences by taking up the law. They perceived, however, how much his cherished ideals would be disturbed by such a course, and generously allowed him his own free choice. About this time his father and mother separated on account of domestic difficulties, the latter settling in Paris, where she died some three years later. Being free to continue his chosen career, Herbart now continued his journey to Bremen, where he spent two years more in preparation for his life-work. Incidentally he tutored a young man for the university, and unfolded his pedagogical ideas to some appreciative mothers belonging to the higher ranks of society. He also wrote several articles and lectures on educational topics. Two of these articles, that on *Pestalozzi's recent work — How Gertrude taught her Children,*[1] and that on *Pestalozzi's Idea of an A B C of Observation,*[2] gave a more scientific form to the thought of the Swiss reformer. The latter essay was afterwards extended by one of Herbart's most important contributions, that on *The Moral or Ethical Revelation of the World the Chief Function of Education,*[3] the most important thought of which is that, through school experiences, and especially through instruction in the common branches, the teacher can reveal the world of moral relations between the individual and his neighbors on the one hand, and organized society on the other, thereby developing a keen moral insight and a right disposition, and insuring reliable moral habits; in a word, developing strong moral character in his pupils. Yet during his stay in Bremen, educational thought was rather a recreation than a serious labor. His chief efforts were expended upon Greek and mathematics. But the question of means wherewith to live began to press upon him, as it has done with many another intellectual benefactor to the world.

[1] Pestalozzi's neueste Schrift: *Wie Gertrud ihre Kinder lehrte.*

[2] Pestalozzi's *Idee eines A B C der Anschauung.*

[3] Ueber die ästhetische Darstellung der Welt als Hauptgeschäft der Erziehung.

As his parents were convinced that philosophy would yield no bread, and were filled with anxiety for his future subsistence, Herbart held it a duty to make no mention of his needs. Not being able to live on air, however, he turned to his friends, especially to Johann Schmidt, with whom he was living, and they out of personal regard and confidence so supplied his wants that he was able to live in a humble way at Bremen, and thence to proceed comfortably to Göttingen. Here, however, his care was increased in a distressing manner. At Jena he had enjoyed good health, and in Switzerland he had become very robust. In stature he was not above middle height; the upper portions of his body were proportionately larger than the lower, so that he was more imposing when sitting than when standing. He was strong and muscular, his movements being decisive and vigorous. But after a long winter journey, in which his emotions were excited to the highest pitch, his health began to fail. He long suffered from 'the baleful effects of the anxieties and over-exertions arising from his state of poverty. During the first years at Göttingen his health was so shattered that he expected every winter to be his last. Yet in spite of these drawbacks, he resolutely pursued his course. Of his academic studies in Bremen but little public record remains. He left with Schmidt two brief essays upon *The Difference between the Idealism of Kant and that of Fichte,* and *A Critique of the Conception of the Ego.*

Upon going to Göttingen he soon qualified as *privat-docent* in pedagogy, not being in touch with the idealistic philosophy of the day. Seeking a firm basis on which to rest his educational theories, he soon began to lecture upon ethics, or practical philosophy. It is said that his lectures were so fine that he soon attracted to his class-room the whole philosophical activity of the university. In consequence of this success he received a call to a full professorship at Heidelberg in 1805, which, however, he declined, though the beautiful spot greatly attracted him.

It is a tribute to the earnestness of philosophic thought of those times that it went on vigorously under the most depressing influences of war and subjugation. Hegel finished his *Phenomenology of Spirit* to the thunder of cannon at Jena, and Herbart out of his slender income was forced to contribute a quota of 1500 francs to the expenses of the war. With Fichte the warmth of philosophic thought burst into flaming zeal for universal education as the surest means of securing national freedom.

During the period of his activity at Göttingen, from 1802 to 1808, Herbart published a number of important works, the principal ones being: A second edition of the *A B C of Observation*, in 1804, to which was added *The Moral Revelation of the World as the Chief Function of Education*. In 1804, was published also *Standpoint for Judging Pestalozzi's Method of Instruction;* in 1806, he issued *General Pedagogics* (his chief work on education), *Chief Points of Metaphysics*, and *Chief Points of Logic*. In 1808 he finished his *General Practical Philosophy*.

The position to which he had attained in Göttingen

was that of extraordinary, or associate, Professor,
with a salary of 300 thalers a year. The alarms of war
and the increasing difficulty of providing sustenance,
gradually led to a diminution of philosophical study
among the students. They drifted largely into more
practical departments, so that when the flattering offer
of Kant's chair at Königsberg, coupled with a salary
of 1200 thalers, came to Herbart, he was ready to
accept it. " How happy I was," he writes, "to receive
the offer of this, the most renowned chair of philosophy, the place which when a boy I longed for in
reverential dreams, as I studied the works of the sage
of Königsberg." [1]

Herbart removed to Königsberg during the spring
of 1809, to occupy the academic chair of Immanuel
Kant, which had just been vacated by Krug, the latter
having accepted a call to Leipsic. During this year
Herbart's father died. " The latter had lived to experience the fact that not only had philosophy supplied his son with bread, but that it had yielded him
honor as well." In addition to lecturing upon philosophy, Herbart was required also to take charge of
pedagogics, which had hitherto been cared for by
several professors, who took turns in lecturing upon
it. In a short time he became personally acquainted
with William von Humboldt, the commissioner of
education for Prussia, who soon appointed Herbart a
member of the school commission having in charge
the interests of higher education. Opposition began
to arise, however, as soon as any serious school reform

[1] *Science of Education*, see Felkins' translation, p. 16.

was urged, the professors dividing into two parties, the young men being mostly for Herbart, and the older professors (who enjoyed certain prerogatives not consistent with the highest welfare of the schools) being opposed to his ideas. All joined heartily with him, however, in the establishment of a pedagogical seminary connected with which was to be a practice school in which a few children should be instructed according to the most scientific methods, and in which the students might participate as instructors under critical observation. Twenty children was the limit set for the practice school, which never, as a matter of fact, however, had more than thirteen members. The parents were required to grant to the teachers the general privileges of private tutors, and were not allowed to interfere with the instruction, at least for one year. The actual teaching was done by from four to six members of the seminary, who at the same time received philosophical and educational instruction in the university. The professor of pedagogy stood in the most intimate relation to the student-teachers, directing, advising, and criticising them. Should a difference of opinion arise between the professor and the student teacher, the latter was required to listen to the advice of the professor, but was not bound to follow it, provided he gave reasons for his own view. Each year the teacher was required to write an educational essay based upon his own experience and observation. This essay was first handed to the professor of pedagogics, who sent it with his comments to the school commissioners. The design was that these student-teachers should become superintendents

of educational institutions upon the completion of
their course.   One of these young men, Karl Volkmar
Stoy, afterwards became the leading exponent of one
school of Herbartians at Jena, where he long conducted a seminary and practice school in accordance
with the plans instituted by Herbart at Königsberg.
The same seminary is now ably continued by Professor William Rein; it is the most noted institution
of the kind in Germany.   The seminary was fully
established in 1810, Herbart lecturing in the university four times a week upon education.

In the house in which he lived, Herbart made the
acquaintance of Mary Drake, the eighteen-year-old
daughter of an English merchant who had been
ruined by the war.   Dr. Bartholomäi, in his biography of Herbart,[1] tells the following anecdote of
their first meeting.   The company were playing cha-
rades, when the name *Herbart* was given.   The first
syllable was described as *a man* (Herr = Mr.), the
second as the *ornament of a man* (bart = beard), and
when the whole was to be characterized, Mary Drake
exclaimed without hesitation, "The whole is the ornament of the university."   Herbart sought the hand
of the young English girl, and they were married.
Their union proved to be a happy one, the wife entering most heartily into the plans and ambitions of her
husband.

The Königsberg period of Herbart's activity was
most fruitful in published works.   The prominence
of his position gave occasion for numerous addresses

[1] *Biography of Herbart*, p. 73.

and minor contributions to philosophy and education, many of which were published. Outside of his metaphysical writings, his most important work was the development of psychology, based anew upon metaphysics, mathematics, and experience. A brief exposition of his psychological ideas and their significance for teaching, is given in the succeeding chapter. His *System of Psychology* was completed in 1814, and his *Text-book of Psychology* in 1816. The main work, however, *Psychology as a Science*, did not appear until 1824–5. His *General Metaphysics* was published in 1828 and 1829 in two volumes, and his *Brief Cyclopedia of Philosophy*, in 1831. The best edition of his pedagogical works is Willmann's scholarly edition in two volumes of about 600 pages each. An English translation of *The Moral Revelation of the World as the Chief Function of Education* and of the *General Principles of Education (Allgemeine Pädagogik)* has been prepared by Mr. and Mrs. Felkin.[1]

Hegel died in 1831, leaving vacant a chair which next to Kant's was the most celebrated in Europe. Herbart fondly hoped to be his successor, and, indeed, there were not a few voices raised in his behalf; but instead of the coveted position, he received an Order. It would have been too much, however, for one man to occupy the vacant places of the two greatest thinkers of modern times. Worthily to have succeeded one of them should have satisfied any reasonable ambition.

But now, restricted by petty officialism, and vexed

[1] Boston: D. C. Heath & Co., 1893.

by misrepresentations, Herbart determined to seek work outside of Prussia, in which the reactionary spirit was dominant. When in 1833, at Schultze's death, Göttingen sought his services, he gladly accepted the call. His time was now fully occupied in preparing and delivering University lectures, so that his published works were few. The students flocked in masses to hear him, often breaking out in cheers. In 1835 he issued *Outline of Pedagogical Lectures,* a work that bears the same relation to his system that Rosenkranz's *Pedagogics as a Science*[1] does to the system of Hegel.

On the 9th of August, 1841, Herbart gave his last lecture with unimpaired ability. Two days afterwards came a stroke of apoplexy that ended his earthly career. His widow lived to see the one hundredth anniversary of his birth. His grave is in Göttingen. It is surrounded by a tall iron fence, inside of which is a cross bearing the following inscription:[2] —

> "To penetrate the sacred depths of truth,
> To strive in joyful hope for human weal,
>   Was his life's aim.
> Now his spirit free hath perfect light,
>   Here rests his mortal frame."

[1] *Philosophy of Education,* by Rosenkranz, with explanatory Paraphrase by Dr. William T. Harris. New York: D. Appleton & Co., 1886.

[2] *Science of Education,* Herbart, Felkins' translation, p. 23.

CHAPTER III

1. CURRENT EDUCATIONAL PSYCHOLOGY

IT is not to the technique of psychology that education looks for guidance, but rather to its point of view and its methods of procedure. The latter are consequently the factors that determine a teacher's professional interest in various psychological systems.

American and English ideas of education are now unquestionably adjusted to a theory of mind that regards our mental constitution from aggregative rather than from organic standpoints. The mind, according to this theory, is an aggregation of faculties; it is the sum of what we call sense-perception, memory, imagination, reason, feeling, choice, volition, and the like. Nor is it sufficient to reply that no real psychologist to-day regards the mind as other than a unit, that these so-called faculties are merely convenient classifications of the methods according to which the mind works; for this does not alter the fact that our educational literature as well as our prac-

23

tice, is completely adjusted to the notion that the
mind is an aggregate of more or less independent
faculties.

In witness of this assertion, we have the frequent
allusion to the training of the faculties, the adjustment of our courses of study in such a way that the
various faculties will receive the appropriate subject-
matter and method of training, as they appear one
by one in the order of their unfolding. Accordingly
we must at first train the senses; whence observation
in the form of the object-lesson becomes a distinct
department of school work; then the memory must
be trained by its appropriate exercise, and must have
a subject-matter adapted to this end. It is well,
therefore, to cram the mind with the largest possible
number of facts in geography, history, and language,
it mattering little whether the facts are concrete or
abstract, related or disparate, interesting or stupid,
since, forsooth, they all train the memory. By and
by, we must, in accordance with this idea, teach
arithmetic because it trains the reason, and so on to
the end of the chapter. That good teachers avoid
these extremes is due, not to the merits of the theory, but to the common sense of the individual.
Curiously enough, we have never introduced anything into the curriculum for the discipline of the
will, though we have made feeble attempts to train
the disposition and to inform the understanding respecting moral relations by teaching somebody's ethical system.

Another natural result arising from considering
the mind as an aggregate of faculties is our favorite

doctrine of mental discipline, or *formal culture* [1] of the intellect. Carried to its logical extreme, this conception assumes, first, that the mind can be well trained with a minimum of concrete knowledge; and, second, that the power gained in one department of knowledge may be transferred unimpaired to any other. An extreme illustration of the first point is that if we train the mind thoroughly upon the abstractions of Greek and Latin grammar, and upon those of pure mathematics, we shall sufficiently culti- vate the faculties; that is, the recipe for developing digestive power is the chewing of rubber, not beef- steak. The second point is commonly urged in dis- cussions upon higher education, where it is usually claimed that a thorough drill on language and mathe- matics will develop a power that can be used with like facility in any department of thought or in any calling in life. A contemplation of the ancient gods portrayed in Homer is just as good a preparation for dealing with the complex industrial forces of the present, as any concrete study of the actual deter- mining conditions, the argument being that the power developed by Greek is like so much mechanical en- ergy, which may be made to do one kind of work as well as another. No one can question the old-time schoolmaster's faith in formal discipline as the main objective end of education, but the world at large refuses to accept this view, evidently regarding for-

[1] Dr. B. A. Hinsdale of the University of Michigan has brought American thought down to date on this subject by his article upon *The Dogma of Formal Culture,* found in the *Educational Review,* September, 1894.

mal training as a myth, or at most as a special preparation for a few professional callings. The public
as a whole insist upon the concrete knowledge studies
for their children, and will pay little for a higher
education that has not visible relations to the activities of life.

The fact that the conclusions of the current educational psychology are not in general accepted by
the people or by scientific students of education, is
sufficient warrant, if one is needed, for the exposition
of a method of thought leading to radically different
educational results.

2. THREEFOLD BASIS OF HERBART'S PSYCHOLOGY

Much of Herbart's psychology is of mere historical
interest, while its more fruitful aspects have under-
gone important changes since his time. In his
thought, psychology has a triple basis, — metaphysics,
mathematics, and experience.

(A.) *Metaphysics — The Soul and its Ideas*

Of Herbart's metaphysical system, in which the
soul as an essence finds a place, we need say but
little. The method of thought is pre-Kantian, rather
than post-Kantian; yet even the metaphysics of psychology has important consequences. The way to
arrive at a sound philosophy, Herbart thought, is to
take the common notions derived from experience
and elaborate them in thought until all their contradictions disappear. Thus, examining the ideas of
substance and quality, we have such difficulties as

these: sugar is *sweet,* is *white,* is *soluble:* What is it that is sweet — the whiteness, the solubility, the weight, and the like? Is the substance the sum of the qualities? is each quality a manifestation of the sum of all the qualities or of all of them except itself? Or is there, on the other hand, a substratum that is not quality or the sum of qualities which yet supports the qualities? If so, what is its nature? How must it be thought? Does it occupy space? Is it, perhaps, a force or system of forces? is it real or ideal? These, and many similar difficulties, must be resolved, if thought is to be made consistent with itself. Herbart's method is to make any assumption whatever that will bring harmony and consistency into our thinking, without regard to the explicability of the assumptions themselves.

Being free, therefore, to make any kind of presupposition whatever regarding the ultimate nature of matter or mind, Herbart constructs an unseen universe as a metaphysical explanation of the seen universe that forms the basis of our experience. From Leibnitz he takes the notion of the monad, or the metaphysical atom, calling it a *real,* at the same time, however, depriving it of its most fruitful principle, that of self-active development. The monad has with Leibnitz no windows or doors through which any outside influence can affect it, all activity, growth, and development coming from within; but Herbart makes the monad single in quality, and aside from a sort of mechanical reciprocity existing among the *reals,* capable of but one kind of activity; namely, the capacity of self-preservation against the annihilation with

which other monads threaten it. The being of the
universe is a plenum of these monads, or *reals*, conceived as in partial interpenetration, and in more or
less mechanical interaction. These monads, or *reals*,
are the noumena of which the events of our experience are the phenomena. As smoke points to fire,
even though the latter is unseen, so the phenomena
of the universe point to a metaphysical substratum,
which we are not at liberty to deny just because it is
not seen. One does not expect, even in the domain of
physical forces, that causes will be *like* their effects.
They are simply adequate to produce them; consequently, it should not appear unthinkable that time-
less and spaceless reals should produce the phenomena
of space and time.

The soul is a monad, doubtless indeed superior to
the myriad other monads with which it is in eternal
interaction. The varying states into which the soul
monad is thrown by its efforts at self-preservation are
ideas. These conditions or states called ideas have
permanent existence in the soul. They appear first
in consciousness, but give place one by one to other
ideas, or acts of self-preservation. Under favorable
conditions they may return again and again to consciousness.

The one important point to note at present respecting this pre-Kantian method of speculation, is that
there is no room in the soul for separate faculties. It
is not a complex, but a simple in which nothing but
ideas, their relations, and interactions exist. The soul
has only ideas, which are its one form of activity;
namely, its self-preservation against other reals. With

this basis, Herbart could confidently declare that his contemporaries had turned psychology into mythology, since they had transformed the various typical internal states of the mind into objective existences called faculties. In his thought, Olympus with its numerous independent gods became the prototype of the psychology which even to-day colors our educational thinking.

But it matters little to us, and is of small consequence for the ultimate validity of Herbart's educational notions, whether this supposed universe of monads, souls included, is a sober reality or a phantasm conjured up by speculation; for his system, after all, depends not upon the constructions of abstract speculation, but upon verifiable facts of experience.

(B.) *Mathematics — Psycho-physics*

If to Herbart's metaphysics we can attribute only indirect or remote influence upon psychology and education, we are justified in ascribing great fruitfulness to the remaining phases of his investigation. As before stated, he sought to form psychology anew upon metaphysics, mathematics, and experience. It is to the second of these that we must now turn.

Though considered in their primary significance, ideas are simply passive states, or "self-preservations of the soul," resulting from the influence of other monads, yet ultimately through their relations to one another these ideas become forces. Some will fuse, or coalesce, partially or completely; some are antagonistic, counteracting or repelling one another;

some are strong, some weak, and none able to sustain themselves for any considerable length of time in consciousness. Ideas, moreover, become associated in series and complications, so that the strong help the weak to reproduction, especially when sense-perception acts as a stimulus to ideas that are below the threshold of consciousness. From all these facts, as well as from the fact that this mental movement persists, whether we will or not, and largely according to laws over which we have no control, Herbart has a warrant for considering ideas as a system of mental forces, whose statics and dynamics may be subjected, ideally at least, to quantitative determination. He therefore applies calculus to mental movement and equilibrium, which, if fanciful in itself, has at least led to important developments in modern psycho-physics and physiological psychology in the hands of such men as Lotze, Fechner, Helmholtz, and Wundt.[1]

(C.) *Experience — Apperception*

But however important for education the quantitative method of psychological study may prove to be, we are not now especially concerned with it, since the specific impulse that Herbart gave to the theory and practice of teaching in Germany has been confined to the remaining aspect of his psychology; namely, that which is founded specifically upon experience, and which has been brought under the general term *apperception*.

[1] A concise account of the development of psychology from the quantitative standpoint is found in Ribot's *German Psychology of To-day*. New York: Charles Scribner's Sons, 1886.

That the assimilative functions of the soul should be the chief study of a psychologist like Herbart is to be expected. So slight an original equipment is assigned to the soul — merely the capacity of self-preservation — that the chief source of its activity must necessarily be experience. The soul becomes enriched with a content, not through the development of any germ-like faculties, but solely through the growth of the ideas that experience creates within us. The attempt of the teacher to train the mind without imparting a thought content is therefore as foolish as was the attempt of the professor in Swift's University of Lagado to extract sunshine from cucumbers. There is no sunshine in cucumbers to extract; and even if there were, it would not repay the labor of extraction. This thought is so subversive of current educational doctrine, that it may be worth while to examine it more closely in order to see precisely what validity it does have. Men do not object upon occasion to readjust their thought, but few are willing to destroy an old system merely for the sake of constructing a new one.

To recognize the importance of Herbart's contributions to educational psychology, it is by no means necessary to accept his metaphysical presuppositions as to the nature and original equipment of the soul. Because experience is a matter of great, not to say supreme, importance in education, it does not follow that nothing else is true or important. Locke, indeed, declares that all the furnishing of our minds has its origin in sensation and reflection, which is perfectly true as to content, but not at all true as to original constitution, unless much is smuggled in under the term *reflection*. Had the mind no original power of activity antecedent to experience, one does not see why a camera should not have perceptions as well as a mind has. Here is the dividing line between the investigations of Kant and Herbart. Though both assume to cover the whole field, each really covers only half. Kant's well-known doctrine of apperception is an investigation into the original constitution of the mind, antecedent to all experience. His constant query is, "What mental equipment must be presupposed in order that perceiving and thinking and willing may be possible?" The content and importance of our perceptions do not enter into his problem. Everything is viewed in its formal aspect, in its validity as a law of activity; nothing is examined as to its concrete worth.

Herbart, on the other hand, neglecting entirely the constitutive equipment of the mind, fixes his attention solely on the production, reproduction, fusion, arrest, and general interaction of ideas. While Kant approaches the study of mind from the critical *a priori* standpoint, Herbart sees only the concrete *a posteriori* side. Apperception with Herbart, therefore, is the assimilation of ideas by means of ideas already possessed, not the Kantian original synthesizing power of the mind.

So far as the educational value of Herbart's theory of concrete apperception is concerned, it is a matter of indifference whether we accept his notions or Kant's as to our original mental constitution, for the teacher has no power to create or to destroy these original powers; he can merely work with what is given. He must, in short, utilize old experience in creating new. His primary function is to impart knowledge in such a way that it can be most rapidly, securely, and profitably assimilated, and this is a problem of concrete apperception. Whether the mind be a germ or a series of germs to be developed, or whether it is a structure to be erected, the process is still the same from the teacher's standpoint. He must know something of the child's previous knowledge and interests in order to utilize them; he must select his material of instruction with respect to ultimate purposes and the pupil's comprehending power; he must arrange the subject-matter not only with respect to the pupil's acquired experience, but also with respect to that which he is going to acquire, i.e., the studies must be brought into the best coördinate relation to one another; and he must adapt his teaching processes so as to secure the quickest apprehension and the longest retention of the matter taught. All this has to do with the acquisition of new experience upon the basis of that already acquired. It matters little, therefore, whether with Herbart we conceive the ideas to be psychical forces, or whether we regard the mind itself as a force or system of forces working upon the ideas as so much passive raw material. The two theories point to the same line of practical activities for the teacher. The advantage is on the Herbartian side, however, since Kant investigates that over which education has no control; namely, the original capacities of the mind, whereas Herbart shows how instruction may best supply and utilize experience. This is precisely the teacher's field of labor. Herein lies the significance of the whole Herbartian school of educational theory and practice. The Herbartians examine all the problems of instruction, school government, and moral training, from the standpoint of a concrete psychology of actual experience. Herbart laid the theoretical foundations; his followers have been and still are engaged in constructing upon these foundations a self-consistent system of educational practice.

Only an illiberal mind would pretend to limit all progress along this line to the tenets of Herbart's specific system of psychology. The point of view is alone important; and this, though ascribed to an individual, is necessarily universal. Any psychology may put the emphasis upon the processes of knowledge and of character growth, rather than upon logical presuppositions or unfruitful distinctions. By doing this it will acquire the essential merits of Herbart's method, retaining, it may be, all of its own specific advantages.

With this general survey of Herbart's psychology in mind, we may turn now to a more specific account of the doctrine of apperception.

Every simple or complex perception (or sensation) which enters consciousness through the gates of the senses, acts as a stimulus upon the ideas possessed by the mind. It repels everything contrary to it that may be in consciousness, and attracts or recalls all similar things, which now rise with all their connections. This complex perception (or sensation) invades several other groups or series simultaneously, and thus induces new conditions of fusion or arrest. While thus it causes a lively movement of ideas, it may be compared to a light casting its rays all around it. The stimulated mass of ideas raised simultaneously may be likened to an arched vault extending in all upward directions from the centre. As long as this arching continues, the central perception has, by virtue of its stimulating power, the controlling influence in consciousness. But the more it checks less similar ideas, which were called up as opposites, the more they recede and allow older, quite similar ideas to rise, and gradually form the apex of the arch; this becomes the more raised or pointed the longer the entire process lasts. Now when a fusion takes place between the new perception (sensation) and the reproduced ideas, which stand high in consciousness, the latter assert and usually maintain a controlling influence, or supremacy. For, as a general rule, the ideas coming from within are, by virtue of their established connections, more potent than the single new percept, especially since the latter diminishes in power as its stimulating effect subsides. The new perception takes the place that its relative importance demands, being made an acquisition of the older series of ideas. In other words, the new element of knowledge is adjusted into the system of ideas already in the mind, and is thus assimilated or apperceived.[1]

Says Lange: "The same relation presupposed between sensations or percepts and older ideas may be

---

[1] Compare Lange's *Apperception*, pp. 256-7 (Boston: D. C. Heath & Co., 1893). This book, translated by the Herbart Club, contains an excellent exposition of the nature and educational significance of the process of apperception, together with a good historical account of the term as used by Herbart, Lazarus, Steinthal, and Wundt.

repeated between the weaker and the stronger ideas that reproduction brings into consciousness. A weaker series of ideas, one that is less deeply rooted within the whole body of thought, may be excited and developed in its own way in the mind. Through its stimulating influence a related mass of thought is reproduced, *i.e.*, one that is stronger and deeper-lying. At first the former, more active series of ideas presses back the second series with reference to its opposing elements. This second series is thus brought to a tension and presses up all the more powerfully. Now it determines the first series in accordance with its own form, holding it by its similar and fusing elements, repelling it at other points." [1]

Herbart develops these ideas at length, and shows moreover the conditions under which apperception most readily takes place. His thought has been much extended and freed from contradictions by his successors, notably Lazarus, Steinthal, and Wundt. Lazarus calls attention to the importance, for apperception, of ideas of which we may for the time be unconscious, as well as of feelings, interests, affections, words, and volitions. In doing this he offers a valuable addition to Herbart's contributions; "for, the forces that in the act of apperceiving awaken and guide the masses of ideas are the secret powers of the emotional soul; to understand them means to recognize the deepest motives and causes of apperception." [2]

Steinthal further develops the theme, classifying the various types of apperception as follows : [3] —

---

[1] Lange's *Apperception*, p. 257.   [2] Ibid. p. 268.
[3] Ibid. pp. 271, 272.

"1. If the object and subject of apperception are perfectly alike, that is, if the impression corresponds to a picture in the memory, both will be fused, not only with reference to the cognition, but also with reference to the conditions of the mind under which the process takes place. This is identifying apperception.

"2. While at times individual things are apperceived by individual ideas, at other times the individual is acquired by the general, the idea of a single being by the idea of the species, the idea of the species by the class, order, and so on. This classifying or subsuming apperception embraces all classifying and arranging, all proving and inferring, all æsthetic and ethical judgment.

"3. Often a definite fact may be classified among certain ideas when one is incapable of harmonizing it with related groups of thoughts that are the seat of lively emotions and desires. When, for instance, a person whom we have loved dies, we understand the event well enough; but we cannot reconcile ourselves with it, cannot bring it into harmony with the condition of the soul; that is, we cannot apperceive it. When at last an adjustment takes place between the opposing groups of ideas, it is not a case of subordination or superiority, but a case of coördination of ideas; that is, the proper relation is found between coördinate ideas or such as belong to different classes. This is the object of harmonizing apperception.

"4. The creative or formative apperception, finally, is found in all those combinations on which the progress of science is based, in the creations of our poets and artists, in the thinking process of induction and deduction, in the guessing of riddles, but also in illusions and hallucinations. There is one characteristic which is peculiarly its own; namely, that in every case it first creates the apperceiving factor."

Wundt's specific contribution to the subject of Apperception is in showing the function of the will in this activity.

Since there is no need of confining this account of Apperception to the initial contribution made by Herbart, the following general summary of the present status of the subject will be in place:[1] (1) The mind must possess an original, inherent power of reacting against the physical stimulus that comes to it through the medium of the senses, else we should never have any experience at all.

The result of this reaction is, ultimately, the production of ideas. Wundt calls this original reacting power the will; since it is the function of the will to manifest its activity in the realm of ideas, the outwardly directed physical effort being an accompanying index. Hence we may say that, in order for knowledge to get a start, the self, in conformity to the will, becomes a necessary element in every sensation, so that if asked, What is a sensation apart from all apperception? we should be compelled to answer, Nothing at all for consciousness, since without apperception we should never have a sensation. This first volitional response of the mind to outward

---

[1] Compare the author's *Essentials of Method*. Boston: D. C. Heath & Co., 1893, pp. 34–36.

physical stimuli coming through the senses, and resulting in sensations and ideas, is *the primary or initial form of apperception*. It is such because it involves no previous knowledge. The phase of apperception most important in education, however, involves knowledge, and may, therefore, be termed the *cognitive apperception*.

(2) To have sensations and ideas, however, is to have what we call consciousness. This may be viewed in two ways. Comparing it figuratively with the image formed upon the retina of the eye in vision, we may distinguish, first, the whole field of illumination, and second, the central focus of light, from which the illumination rapidly diminishes to the periphery of the image. If we call all activity within the *field* of consciousness *perception*, then the activity within the *focus* of consciousness, or the point of greatest clearness, may be distinguished by the name *apperception*.

(3) The elements of mental life, as they are presented by the senses, have a varying value in consciousness, those of most subjective worth coming into the focus, and others remaining in outlying portions of the field. The primal activity of the mind in responding to these stimuli has been called the will, so that the ideas that get into the focus of consciousness must have the greatest momentary worth to the will. But that which has value in relation to the will is a *motive*, so that we may speak of the soliciting power that an idea has for the will as its *motive value*. This changes from moment to moment and from stage to stage in the development of the mind. What is a strong motive to us at one

time or in one condition ceases to be such at another
time, or when the state of the mind has changed.[1]

(4) It is because the original activity of the mind
in its response to sense stimuli is conceived as will,
that it is proper to regard the worth that each idea
has for the mind as a *motive value*. This value is to
be expressed in terms of feeling, whether having
its origin in the body or in the contemplation of
intellectual or moral truths. To have the motive
value arising from perceived knowledge relations, an
idea must enter the field of consciousness, when it
may be quickly elevated into the focus, provided it
possesses enough motive value. This will depend,
not so much upon its actual value considered in itself,
as upon the subjective worth it has for a mind that
is constantly changing its tone in obedience to alter-
ing content of consciousness. We may say, in general,
that the motive value of an idea at any given time
will depend upon the worth the idea appears to have
for the well-being of the self. It may range from
the satisfaction of the simplest physical want arising
from the bodily organism, up to the realization of the
impulses of the self in the loftiest realms of intellectual and moral life.

(5) Though the mind through its will activity
(power of "self-preservation," Herbart would say)
creates ideas, it does so in obedience to stimuli coming from sources independent of itself. On this
account the original content of mental life depends

[1] That this view of the will is not Herbart's, will be seen later in
the present chapter. It is by no means the Kantian conception,
however, since it is primarily determined by ideas.

in large degree upon causes over which the mind has no control, but it may be said that all ideas have been more or less perfectly apperceived before they are recognized as old and familiar. Recurring ideas that have been apperceived are recognized as such, and no longer command the attention necessary to bring them to the focus of consciousness, unless they possess a motive value sufficient to call for a more complete apperception. They, it may be said, usually constitute the main body of ideas in the field of consciousness — they are perceptions which may, however, be called into the focus at any moment.

(6) New ideas entering consciousness, whether occasioned by physical or psychical processes, usually possess a sufficient motive value to raise them into the apperceiving centre. They can obtain significance, however, only when they are consciously related to other ideas. In order to establish these relations, the mind must hold in the focus of its attention, not only the newly entering idea, but also those to which it is to be related. The impossibility of holding one of two related ideas in the focus of consciousness, and keeping the other in the background at the moment of establishing the relation, seems to substantiate this view. We may say, therefore, that in an ordinary act of apperception the mind holds under the focus of its attention, not only the new notion, but also the other ideas to which it must be related in order to have significance.

One of the most distinctive features of recent Herbartian thought is that all instruction, even in what we regard as non-moral subjects, such as science, mathematics, linguistics, profane history, and litera- ture, should tend directly and powerfully to the forma- tion of moral, not to say religious, character. If this view has more than a sentimental validity, it is worthy of the most serious attention; for it is evident to every thoughtful man that our public schools have been intellectualized beyond what is best for the in- dividual, and the general moral welfare. In our anx- iety that the schools should not become sectarianized we have allowed them to become secularized to an unwarrantable extent. Nothing, therefore, could be more welcome to the friends of public education, than a system of school training that will tend strongly to develop the moral character, without having recourse to conflicting religious doctrines. Such a system, the Herbartians claim to offer. It remains for us briefly to examine its psychological basis.

A logical consequence of our "faculty" psychology is the notion that the will is potentially free, that any man can do as he pleases irrespective of circum- stances and education. This is a convenient doctrine while we are administering a criminal code, but it is not stimulating to the teacher, either as an induce- ment to try to educate a child into goodness, or as an indication of his ability to do so. The first arraign- ment that Herbart makes of Kant's intelligible or transcendental freedom, is that a will which is inde- pendent of experience except in capacity to control experience, cannot be educated. If we will, we will; if we won't, we won't; and that is an end of the whole matter. The Bible injunction, "Train up a child in the way he should go, and when he is old he will not depart from it," has no applicability to a will that sits serene and high above the influences of space and time. Transcendental or original and absolute freedom of will is accordingly inconsistent with the idea of moral education.

Here again we must assume the judicial attitude and inquire into the validity of these notions. While Kant, on the one hand, was so busied with *a priori* phase of mind that he took no time to show how this potential moral freedom might become actual through experience, or to distinguish sufficiently between the mechanical freedom of caprice (which in the end is no freedom at all) and that rational freedom which is founded on the highest morality; so Herbart, on the other, hampered perhaps by his metaphysical presuppositions, and engrossed with the *a posteriori*, or practical, side of the problem, emphasizes solely the development of character through the concrete growth of knowledge and ideals. This again is the domain of the teacher; for no more in character than in intellect does he make or unmake the original powers of the soul: he can only develop ideals through ideas. It is, therefore, a matter of indifference to the teacher whether the mind has this absolute freedom or not, since in either event it must have the same education. Again Herbart has the advantage, as in the intellectual realm, for he deals with character as a growth.

Since, according to Herbart, the soul possesses nothing but ideas, it became necessary for him to explain those states which we call feeling, desire, and voli-

tion without the aid of any innate mental machinery.
Feeling is represented as arising from the relation of
ideas. "A feeling is the consciousness of a furthering or an arrest of the movement of thought: when
a furthering, a feeling of pleasure; when an arrest, a
feeling of pain. The life of the soul is one of ideas;
every furthering of them is at the same time a promotion of the life activity of the mind; every arrest
of ideas is also an arrest of soul life." [1]

"Desire is in general a state of mind which strives
to bring about some other state of mind not now present. It is always directed toward some particular
object; but of course only the idea of the object, not
the object itself, can penetrate to consciousness — not
gold, for instance, but the idea of undisturbed possession; not the water, but the sensation of satisfied
thirst. Yet the idea of the object is already in consciousness when desired. He who does not know the
quenching power of water, or who cannot imagine
the pleasure of its possession, would never desire it.
Before possession, the idea is arrested, afterward it is
freed from arrest. Impulse strives, therefore, to shake
off the undesirable state of arrest from the idea of
the desired object, and to exchange this state for that
of freedom from arrest in order to be complete master of the object so far as can be through the medium
of ideas." [2]

"But desire, in accordance with its idea, seeks satisfaction. If this appears impossible, the impulse remains mere wish, and has no further significance; but

[1] Lindner, *Empirical Psychology* (Boston: D. C. Heath & Co.,
1889), p. 170.   [2] Lindner, Ibid. p. 213.

if to the desire there is added a belief in the attainability of the desired object, the desire passes into will and reveals itself in action and deeds. An object of desire is attainable when it appears as the final member of a series of changes which are related as cause and effect, the first member of the series proceeding from the ego that wills. If such a causal series comes to the support of any desire, the desire is transformed into will; the object is not only desired, it is willed. Will means, then, the desire for a certain result and the certainty, or at least a *belief* in the certainty, of its attainment. The impossible may be willed as soon as it appears to us as possible; and for the same reason we may desire without willing that which is really possible and practicable, so long as we are lacking in insight as to ways and means of reaching it. The clearer the insight as to the attainability of an object, the more conscious a man is that he can attain what he desires, the stronger his will is." [1]

According to this view our will activities are the natural accompaniments and logical conclusions of our thinking; *i.e.*, they result from the content and relations of our ideas. Character-building is will-training, and this in turn is the apperception of ideas. Reversing the order, the teacher imparts ideas in such order and manner as to secure their proper apperception; also so that transient and permanent desires shall awaken from them, which in turn seek their satisfaction in the deeds arising from volition. The question of absolute freedom is one of metaphysics, not of pedagogics. The teacher is concerned alone with that psychological freedom whose development he can direct and stimulate, if not actually determine. Furthermore, since the great mass of volitions that man has occasion to execute pertain to his relations to nature and his fellow-men both as individuals and as organized in institutions, it follows that these volitions arise naturally from the ideas that the school imparts, such as those pertaining to science, history, literature, civil government, and economics. All that need be left to the Church is the cultivation of adequate emotional and intellectual attitude towards specific systems of religious doctrine. Subsequent chapters will show the direction along which the followers of Herbart have sought to make all the activities of the schoolroom focus in the development of moral character.

CHAPTER IV

HERBART'S ETHICS — A GUIDE TO EDUCATIONAL ENDS

THE mere exposition of a system of ethics might, in a work of this sort, prove to be of small interest, yet so great is the emphasis laid upon this department of philosophy as a guide to teaching, not only by Herbart, but by all his adherents, that any account of his educational contributions would be very defective were the subject passed over in silence. The idea that the deeper purpose of education is the development of moral character rather than intellectual acumen is by no means new. Centuries ago Socrates maintained the teachableness of virtue, claiming that right doing is the necessary result of complete knowing. As we have seen in the preceding chapter, Herbart finds the roots of volition in the ideas arising from the various sources of experience. Moral insight gained from a moral revelation of the world as it is effected, partly through home experience, but chiefly through school instruction, may easily pass into moral ideas through cultivation of a right spirit or disposition. By means of careful oversight and discipline tempered by love, moral ideals may become permanent rules of action through the formation of reliable moral habits. That is to say, moral character is a growth arising from the soil of experience as gained through knowledge and social intercourse, not a mystical faculty born in us.

In order, therefore, to develop moral ideals and to transform them into rules of life through a moral revelation of the world, the teacher must have a clear consciousness of the fundamental ethical ideas, or moral principles, that find their embodiment in conduct.

Herbart's theory of the manner in which we arrive at moral judgments may or may not satisfy the mind of the student; yet this is a matter of small consequence, for all ethical systems arrive at substantially the same rules of life, however varied the derivation of these principles may be. The important thing for the teacher is to see how these ethical results can be utilized in education to secure moral insight and disposition. To the solution of this problem Herbart makes the following contribution: —

Feelings are states of the mind arising from the relations of ideas. Certain harmonious relations give rise to inevitable feelings of pleasure, and their opposites give us equally inevitable feelings of displeasure or pain. From this fact our moral judgments arise, just as our judgments of harmony or discord in music arise. We do not ask why a certain combination of tones pleases; we decide that it does. In the same manner we condemn a discord. Morality necessarily has to do with the will, since only this can be good or bad. Herbart addressed himself to the task of mak-

ing a final reduction of all possible will relations, in
order thus to arrive at the irreducible moral or ethical conceptions. In this way he arrived at five moral
ideas, two of which are formal in their nature, and
three concrete. Each of the ideas is valid in its individual and in its institutional aspects; that is, between
man and man and between the individual and the
organized groups of society, such as the family, the
school, the civil community, the state or nation, and
the coöperative groups of business. The ideas in
detail are as follows: —

1. The Idea of Inner Freedom

This idea arises from an inner relation between our
deeds and our insight as to what is right or wrong;
that is, between volition and ideas. It is founded on
the pleasure arising from inner harmony. If the two
are in accord, then the mind is at peace with itself,
the conscience approves. A man who has deliber-
ately acted in accordance with his firm belief as to
what is right is internally or subjectively free. His
conscience approves, and he is at peace with himself,
even though at war with others. The teacher rightly
tries to cultivate the conscientious spirit, but it is no
less his duty to inform the understanding as to the
moral relations that are valid in the world, and to
enlist the interests and affections of the mind in
their behalf.

2. The Idea of Efficiency of Will

This idea also is formal, but of great consequence.
It implies, first, a certain positive force of determina-

tion and vigor of execution.   Everybody knows what
a weak will is, and how hopeless is the case of a man
who cannot be counted upon to reduce his good reso-
lutions to practice.   The efficient will is the strong
will.   But it is more.   It must, also, be reasonably
concentrated in its action; that is, it must make all
its efforts work together for the accomplishment of
leading purposes.   All this, however, is purely formal,
and holds of evil as well as of good men.   No man
can be *positively* bad whose will is not strong and
concentrated.   A truly efficient will, however, must
be consistent in its main lines of action, and to be
consistent it must be right; for deeds that are consis-
tently evil are wholly self-destructive in the end,
whilst there can be no idea of really efficient volitional life where one action contradicts its fellow,
as must be the case where one's deeds are partly
right and partly wrong.   It appears to follow, therefore, that to be truly efficient one's will must be
strong, concentrated, and consistent with the real
ethical order of the world.   But even granting that
a will cannot be efficient that is not rightly directed,
the fact still remains that this principle is purely
formal, since it throws no light on what is right or
wrong.   The basis of this idea is the pleasure we
have in the perfection of power.

3. The Idea of Good-will

It is the natural impulse of each individual to make
himself the end and center of all that he comes in
contact with, to make himself the master to which

everything else must be subordinate. This is a natural impulse, because each self is in reality the center to which all its own mental experiences must be related. But this same experience soon teaches him that there are other selves with claims equal to his own, and that if he would have his own selfhood respected, he must respect that of others. There thus arises practically in the world the idea that Christianity calls *Good-will*. It is that state of mind in which the validity of a foreign *ego* is recognized, or in which the good of another is willed as if *for* self. Its opposite is ill-will, a feeling whose impulse is to injure or destroy or subordinate a foreign *ego*. Good-will is the key to a long list of virtues, such as kindness, benevolence, charity, fidelity, goodness, generosity; while its opposite, ill-will, gives rise to an equally extended list of faults. Exercise of the virtues of good-will pleases us unconditionally, while a manifestation of their opposite meets our unquestioning disapprobation.

4. The Idea of Justice, or Prevention of Strife

The idea is founded on our natural displeasure in contention. It comes to light when two individuals strive for the possession of that which, in the nature of the case, only one of them can have. It is the idea of *rights*, which lies at the basis of most of our laws regarding property. A large part of the judicial system of every country is devoted to the securing of justice in the acquisition, possession, and disposition of wealth.

5. The Idea of Equity or Requital

This idea arises whenever existing will-relations are altered either for good or bad. It is the notion of requital for good or bad actions, and it demands that the requital shall be adequate to the deed. This idea is the basis of the system of rewards, and especially of punishments, that society has gradually evolved. Institutionalism takes the requital of evil deeds out of the hands of the injured person, and places it in those of the state. The effect is to ward off from others the blow of the evil-doer, making it return upon his own head. This conception is expressed in Michael Angelo's *Last Judgment*, where each shows by his looks that he is but facing the result of his own deeds, which carry their own requital with them.

Such, Herbart thought, are the root-ideas of moral life. It is the business of education to keep them in touch with instruction throughout its course, to make them the guide to social intercourse, and the disciplinary requirements of the school. In this way the child may reap the benefit of the accumulated experience of the past, just as he inherits the wealth stored up by his immediate ancestors. In the impressionable years of childhood and youth, while the heart is tender, the imagination vivid, and the apprehension quick, it is possible so to enlist these faculties that the moral victory may be won before the real battle is fought. We do not hesitate to have the child enter into the inheritance that the past has left us in knowledge. No child is asked to start a thousand years behind his time in any great field of human endeavor.

Our children now accept the electric light as freely as our grandfathers did the oil lamp or the tallow candle. The same is true in every realm of science and practical life. We seize the advantage gained, and go on to new conquests. Why should it be otherwise in the moral world? Why may not the bitter lessons of the past in the struggle with ethical principles be turned quite as fully to account as the results in the intellectual world? What a weary round of scourgings the race has gone through to arrive at its present state of material, political, and moral freedom! The child is born now, as ever, with all his experiences before him. Must he, for want of proper education, retrace the thorny path of his forefathers? We do not ask it with regard to his material or intellectual welfare. Why should we with the moral?

Not only do the five ethical ideas pertain to individuals as such, but as we have seen they have also an institutional bearing. Thus the fifth idea, that of equity, gives rise in society to a system of rewards of a negative kind; that is, punishments for the disturbance of ethical balance. If a rich man offers the life-guard a nickel for rescuing him from the ocean breakers, our moral sense is outraged, but the law inflicts no penalty; but if one person defrauds another of property or of some personal right legally his due, then the law prescribes penalties. On behalf of the idea, Justice, society institutes a legal code, together with a legal machinery for the hindrance of strife. The business of the lawyer should be as much the prevention of contention as the establishment of equity. Furthermore, in order to realize the idea of Good-will in its institutional aspects, society organizes a system of administration aimed at the greatest possible good of all. To make all wills efficient so far as may be, society sustains a system of culture in its schools, colleges, and universities aimed at the greatest possible power and efficiency. Finally, the idea of inner freedom in the large sense involves the conception of the state as a personality having a volition, or power of acting, and a constitution, together with its accompanying statutes. As an individual, the state is free when its actions and its laws are in harmony; progress is secured by the gradual change of fundamental or statute law through legislation. When the legal status of the nation collides with the ethical ideas that rule the individual (slavery, for instance, compelled men to refrain from natural impulses of good-will, as in obeying the fugitive slave law), then a conflict arises between the conscience of the individual and the constitution of the state. This discord continues until the conscience is seared or the constitution altered.

Grasping the ideas together in their individual and in their institutional bearings, we have for the individual the conception of *virtue*. Virtue, therefore, involves goodness, clear conscience, efficiency of will, justice and equity in private and in public life.

There is a double reason why Herbart's thought of moral training is important for us. In the first place, the public schools are debarred from any sectarian use of the Bible as well as from all religious ceremonial, because of the simple fact that these schools are for all sects. It is, therefore, practically impossible for them to make distinctively religious doctrine the

basis of their moral training, however desirable such
a procedure may be deemed. In the next place, it
should be recognized that the moral problem in its
concrete filling changes from age to age. The Golden
Rule has indeed eternal validity, but the deeds that I
would that my neighbor should do to me differ with
the changing ideals of different ages. Furthermore,
ideals of morality arising from the relations of individuals to society as grouped into civil, social, educational, charitable, and family organizations are subject to still wider variations. In ancient Greece, moral
conceptions were focussed about the art ideal. In
Rome, the boys were taught to swim (that the Roman
armies might not be stopped by rivers) and to know the
table of the laws. Thus virtue was first æsthetic, then
military and civil in its essence. During the Middle
Ages, when the Church was both the spiritual and the
temporal power that ruled the world, morality necessarily fused with the religious idea, hence obedience
to church authority and strict conformity to her or-
dained ceremonial was naturally esteemed the basis of
moral character. In our own age, however, science
and political evolution have changed the point of view.
In theory, at least, every individual has political
freedom and equality. All are alike in the liberty to
influence the social, educational, economic, and political policy of the nation. Science has at the same
time made it possible for many more people to live
much better. Not only are larger populations now
possible, but public hygiene and medical science enable
even the feeble to survive; civil equality has raised
the demand for universal education, and this in turn

lifts the ideals of the people as to what belongs of right to human existence — a high standard of life — good, wholesome food — decent shelter and clothing — and some leisure. The scholar has long been able to make his recreations conduce to the vigor of his body; the laborer now demands leisure to make his recreations contribute to the cultivation of his mind. In spite, therefore, of the fact that there is much in morality that is unchanging and eternal, the emphasis, perpetually changing, is now economic, social, and civil, as it was once æsthetic, then military, then ecclesiastical. Who that contemplates modern society with its few masters and many men, its concentration of capital and division of labor, its strikes, its lockouts, its bloody encounters, and its systems of arbitrations, can doubt that the institutional phases of morality are different from what they were in the past? Universal political liberty has also brought new problems, which in our great cities are sharply accented, while the advancing moral sense of the people reveals in new light the bane of intemperance and social impurity. With this prohibition of the use of religious doctrine as the basis of moral teaching, on the one hand, and the growing importance of what we may term public or institutional morality on the other, we may the more warmly welcome the thought of Herbart that school discipline and instruction in the common branches, if illumined by the fundamental moral ideas, may be the adequate means for developing moral character. The thought that there may thus be a moral revelation of the world to the child through discipline and instruction in the school will be more fully exemplified in subsequent chapters.

CHAPTER V

THE DOCTRINE OF INTEREST — ITS BEARING UPON KNOWLEDGE AND VOLITION

A complete chapter on the subject of Interest would be an exposition of the greater part of Herbart's theory of instruction. Indeed, the caption *Many-sided Interest* is used throughout his discussion of that topic. Ziller in his *Grundlegung* devotes two hundred and nine pages to an elaboration of the educational significance of the idea. All Herbartian writers attach great importance to the subject, for reasons which will now be briefly stated.

The Herbartian psychology rejects as a pure myth the idea that there is in the human mind any independent, or transcendental, faculty whose function is to will, and which is free in the sense that it can originate actions that are independent of all ideas or of thought processes. On the contrary, with Herbart's system, volition is strictly dependent upon ideas, — a product of them either as they originally appeared in the mind, or as they have come to be through repeated returns to consciousness. Ideas become adjusted into apperceiving masses, with which are associated interests, desires, and volitions. A volition is therefore only an idea which has passed through a complete development, of which interest is an essential stage. That being the case, it becomes of the greatest importance that the child should conceive an inherent, abiding, and growing interest in the subject-matter through which instruction is expected to furnish a moral revelation of the world. Unless the teacher can succeed in exciting such an interest, he cannot make knowledge yield more than an intellectual theoretical morality, which is perhaps little better than none. The teacher desires that *ideas* of virtue should develop into *ideals* of conduct; he hopes that the heart will be warmed for these ideals; but of such a consummation there is small prospect so long as the child regards the content of his studies with indifference, it may be with aversion. Instruction cannot, therefore, remain a dry, perfunctory drill upon forms of knowledge and accomplish its highest mission. We see now why all Herbartians make so much of apperception, or the assimilation of ideas through ideas; why they insist that the subject-matter shall be selected, arranged, articulated, and presented in strict accordance with the stores and processes of the children's minds. Only in this way can knowledge become rich in meaning to the pupil, revealing ever-widening relations to life and conduct.

We often conceive of interest in study merely as a means for securing attention to lessons, hoping that the knowledge will remain after the interest has departed; whereas, the other conception is that through a proper presentation of the right amount of knowledge in the best manner and at the right time,

we may incite an interest that will abide even after
the knowledge has faded from the mind. Each of
these conceptions of interest has a certain validity,
but the latter goes much deeper; it is one of the
abiding results that instruction should reach. A
harmoniously developed, many-sided interest of this
sort is, on the one hand, a sort of graduated scale by
which we may measure the success of our efforts as
educational artists; and, on the other, the grand
initial stage in the formation of moral character
through the development of ideals, the cultivation of
moral disposition, and the acquisition of moral habits.
We see a new reason for rejecting the doctrine of
formal culture of the mind as a desirable educational
process. The moral world is not fully revealed
through language and mathemetics, even when these
are as concrete as possible, much less when they are
formal and abstract.

The following quotation from Kern[1] shows that
interest is regarded, not alone from the standpoint of
temporary expediency, but from that of its bearing
upon the future of the individual: "In a many-sided
interest the pupil should find a moral support and
protection against the servitude that springs from
the rule of desire and passion. It should protect
him from the errors that are the consequence of idle-
ness; it should arm him against the fitful chances
of fortune; it should make life again valuable and
desirable even when a cruel fate has robbed it of
its most cherished object; it should enable one to find

[1] Kern, *Grundriss der Pädagogik*, 12.

a new calling when driven from the old; it should elevate him to a standpoint from which the goods and successes of earthly striving appear as accidental, by which his real self is not affected, and above which the moral character stands free and sublime."

That the subject of interest should be regarded specifically also, Herbart divided the various kinds of interests into two groups or classes; namely, (*a*) interests arising from knowledge, and (*b*) interests arising from intercourse with others, as in the family, the school, the church, the civil community, society.

(A.) Interests from Knowledge

Of interest as related to knowledge, we may distinguish the following phases : —

1. The empirical interest, or the pleasure excited in the mind by the changes and novelty that arise from a presentation of the manifold and variegated. Wonder is one of its manifestations, and is, as Plato long ago told us, the starting-point of knowledge. The exciting of empirical interest is, therefore, the beginning of education; it explains many of the devices of the kindergarten, and most of the concrete objective work of the primary school. A large part of the devices regarded as methods of teaching are invented to catch the wandering attention of the children until it can be fixed on more serious things. These devices are perfectly legitimate, and even necessary, unless, passing their proper limit, they become hysterical or sensational. One sometimes finds schools in which the children will ignore every-

thing but the most dramatic efforts to attract their attention, and will give but transient heed even to these. That every earnest purpose of education is thereby destroyed at least for the time being is self-evident.

2. The speculative interest, or the search for the causal connection of things to which the dark, or problematical, or mysterious impels the mind.[1] "He who rejoices upon looking into the starry heavens has the empirical interest; he who reflects upon the conditions of stellar origin has the speculative interest." It is the speculative interest to which we appeal when we teach pupils to perceive the reasons of things; when we lead them to look beyond the facts to the laws that unify them, and make them appear in their rational connection. This interest is of the utmost importance for education. Its beginnings are found in very young children, and not until a mind has become atrophied by age or occupation or bad teaching does it cease to be the mainspring of intellectual life. So long as spontaneity remains, the causal and other rational relations of things will be sought. It is in the discovering of these relations that thinking chiefly consists. It needs no argument, therefore, to demonstrate that an interest so vital to mental vigor should be developed to the fullest extent by the teacher. The man is intellectually dead whose mind is not continually challenged to investigation, who like the stolid ox plods on, unmindful of all that does not promise to minister directly to his

---

[1] Ufer, *Introduction to the Pedagogy of Herbart*, translated by J. C. Zinser. Boston: D. C. Heath & Co., 1894.

physical profit. How can a man be a good citizen who cares nothing for the causes that produce misrule in the land? How can he be a useful brother who cares nothing for the social and economic forces that produce weal or woe to his fellows? What to him are railroads, steamships, telegraphs, newspapers, and all the great instruments of industry, if he is not stimulated by their presence to investigate their function? The Macbeths of the mind are those who silence its cry for the knowledge of origin and causes. The speculative interest is the gateway to all progress that rests on the apprehension of logical relations.

3. The æsthetic interest, or that which is aroused not by the manifoldness and variety of things or their causal relations, but the contemplation of an *ideal* through a *sense* medium, as, for instance, the *character* of Moses (an ideal) through Michael Angelo's *statue* of him (made of marble). It is the interest aroused by the beautiful in nature, in art, or in morals. In the case of moral beauty, an ideal is manifested, not through stone or canvas, but by means of conduct — action. This interest — a passionate one with most persons of some races, and with some persons among all races — is often neglected through contempt for its utility or fear of its influence. That art has sometimes been debased to ignoble uses is no more an argument for its neglect, than the fact that religion has often been used to inflame hatred is a reason for its abandonment. The soul has a right to symmetrical development; but this it cannot have if a part of its natural inter-

ests are ignored. It must therefore be asserted, in spite of Puritan teaching to the contrary, that the æsthetic sense of the children must be cultivated as the source of much pure joy. The time should come when even the artisan will be an artist in his work, when beauty will be everywhere a sweetener of life. To these ends, as well as to the idea of beauty as an end in itself, the teacher must turn a part of his attention.

(B.) INTERESTS ARISING FROM ASSOCIATION WITH OTHERS

Of the interests arising from human relations, the following points may be distinguished: —

1. The sympathetic interest, or that which is aroused by the joy or sorrow of others. The cultivation of this species of interest should begin in the family, though as a matter of fact it is very frequently repressed by a collision of selfish wills, giving rise to all sorts of bickerings and petty heartburnings. It often happens, therefore, that children first learn in the kindergarten what satisfaction there is in the spirit of coöperation. Miss Harrison of Chicago relates an incident of a pretty young miss who came to the kindergarten dressed in silks and spangles. The children began a play in which the girls were to represent the housewives and the boys the out-of-door laborers. When the part of preparing dinner for Tommy came to the new pupil, she flung herself into a chair with many airs, saying, "My mamma doesn't get dinner; she leaves that for the servants." "Very well," said the teacher, "we

will excuse you, if you like." The play went on with much pleasure to all except the little girl in silks, who sat debarred from all the fun. The next day she dismissed her foolish pride, and, after that, entered heartily into all the occupations of the kindergarten. The school, too, has constant opportunity to develop the spirit of brotherly kindness, ideally in such studies as literature, history, zoölogy; really in the daily intercourse of the pupils.

If this feeling of individual sympathy is extended by a knowledge of the wider relations of society into feelings respecting the welfare of large numbers, we have : —

2. The social interest. It is in laying the foundations for this species of interest that the kindergarten is preëminent. Its games, plays, songs, occupations, involving the coöperation of all the members, are an ideal epitome of social coöperation in its highest form. The school should continue to develop the spirit so admirably generated in the kindergarten, for out of these beginnings grow the great institutional interests of the Anglo-Saxon race. It lies at the basis of public spirit, charity, public reform, patriotism, commercial reciprocity, and their kindred virtues. The studies that give preëminent opportunity for the development of this interest are literature, civics, and commercial geography. This last study, more than any other, reveals to the child his own present and possible future relation to the business world. Even the barefooted urchin of the country crossroads may be led to see that his parents cast their mite into the world's commerce to have it returned to

them, not after many days, but at once, enriched and magnified. The heart of the youth is fired as he beholds the possibilities of a life of coöperative harmony with others; he sees the possibilities of his own worth enhanced a thousand fold, his petty selfhood infinitely enlarged, his dignity exalted, through the reinforcement that the race brings to him when he learns the supreme lesson of serving himself through service to his fellow-man.

3. The religious interest. This interest may be to considerable extent awakened in the school, even when not a word is said about the subject in the form of direct instruction. As Ufer says, " When interest is directed to the history and destiny of mankind, when it is as clear to the understanding as to the feelings that the ordering of the history of man involves something more than mere human power, and that, therefore, the history of each individual does not lie entirely in his own hands, then fear and hope gather in the heart." [1]

The foregoing exposition is designed to show that Herbart meant by interest something of vast importance to the development of the individual, not a mere tickling of the mind for transient ends. In the words of Staude, " Interest is the light with which Herbart has once for all brought the dark and tortuous course of didactics into the clearness of day. It is the charmed word which alone gives power to instruction to call the spirit of youth and to make it serve the aim of the master. It is the lever of

[1] Ufer, *Introduction to the Pedagogy of Herbart*.

education, which, lightly and joyfully moved by the teacher, can alone bring the youthful will into the desired activity and direction." [1]

[1] Dr. R. Staude, *Pädagogische Studien*, Hrsg. von W. Rein, Heft II.

CHAPTER VI

INSTRUCTION — ITS MATERIALS, COURSE, AND METHOD

1. MATERIALS OF INSTRUCTION

THE materials of instruction are the literature and science that constitute human knowledge. It is to Herbart's successors that one must look for detailed directions for the selection and articulation of the subject-matter of instruction. Herbart himself discussed these topics for the most part in principle only. Of literature and history he says. "Periods which no master has described, whose spirit no poet breathes, are of little value to education." [1] Guided by the doctrine of apperception as an index to the child's natural interests, he insisted that Greek should come before Latin. He found his boys ready and eager to read the Odyssey at a period at which Latin was highly distasteful to them. The following testimony as to his own experience gives his point of view :

"I am indebted to the Odyssey for one of the happiest experiences of my life, and in a great degree for my love of education. This experience did not teach me the motive ; *that* I saw before, clearly enough to

[1] Herbart, *Science of Education*, Felkins' translation, p. 74.

begin my work as a teacher by allowing two boys, one nine, the other not yet eight years old, to lay their Eutropius aside, and requiring from them Greek instead, even Homer at once, without any so-called preparation by the hotch-potch of text-books. I erred in keeping far too closely to the routine of schools, exacting accurate grammatical analysis, when for this beginning only the principal signs of inflection ought to have been taught and explained with untiring repetition, rather than demanded again and again from the boy by pressing questions. I lacked all preparation in history and mythology, so necessary to make exposition easier, and so easily furnished by a student who possesses true educational tact. Many an injurious breeze from afar disturbed me much in my surroundings, which, I can now but silently think, was favorable to me. But nothing can destroy my hope that the good natures of healthy boys are not to be considered such rarities, but will stand the greater number of educators in good stead as they stood me. And while I can easily imagine a much greater art in carrying out the task than my first attempt can boast, I believe I learned from my experience (for which the reading of the Odyssey required a year and a half) that this commencement in private tuition is as practicable as it is wholesome, and that it must ordinarily succeed in this sphere, if teachers who approach the subject not only in the philological but also in the educational spirit, will lay down some rules by way of help and foresight, more minutely than time and space at present permit me to do. I cannot determine what is possible in schools, but were I in the position to do so, I would make the attempt with courage, and with the firm conviction, that even if the result were failure, the evil could not be greater than arises from the customary study of Latin grammar and Roman authors, of which not one exists even passably suitable for guiding a boy at any period of his childhood into the ages of antiquity. They may conveniently follow, if Homer and a few other Greeks have gone before. But a considerable amount of learned confusion is shown in the manner in which they have hitherto been used, and in tolerating for the sake of an instruction so wholly wanting in all educational value, so much labor for so many years, so much sacrifice of good humor, and of all free movement of the mind. I appeal to many educational reviews more easily forgotten than confuted, which at any rate exposed this great evil, even if they did not at once point out a suitable remedy.

"The preceding is sufficient to afford a preliminary acquaintance with this proposal; it is *not* sufficient to exhibit it in its infinitely numerous relations. It would be but a beginning, were any one inclined to grasp the whole of the present volume in one thought, and carry that thought about with him for many years. I at least have not given expression hurriedly to my experience. My attempt began more than eight years ago, and since then I have had time to consider it.

" Let us rise to a general consideration of the subject. Let us look on the Odyssey as the point of touch in a fellowship between pupil and teacher, which, while it elevates the one in his own sphere, no longer depresses the other, and while it guides the one farther and farther through a classical world, yields the other a most interesting picture in the imitative progress of the boy, of the great development of humanity, and lastly prepares a store of recollections, which, associated with this eternal work of genius, must be reawakened at each return to it. In like manner, a familiar star recalls to friends the hours when they were wont to observe it together." [1]

Further directions as to choice of material are given in the *Science of Education*,[2] as follows : —

" Without wasting time I merely mention that of Homer's works, the cruder Iliad is not suitable, but the entire Odyssey is, with the exception of a single long piece in the eighth book (individual expressions can be easily avoided). The Philoctetus of Sophocles in early years, then the historical writings of Xenophon (not, however, the essentially immoral Memorabilia, which owe their reputation to the greatest-happiness doctrine), and in later boyhood, after a few easy Dialogues, the Republic of Plato can be read. This last is exactly suited to the awakening interest in wider society ; in the years when young men seriously devote themselves to politics it is just as little satisfying as Homer to a youth who is just at that period when he throws everything childlike behind him. Plato, as the teacher of idealism, and Homer, as the poet, always remain for riper age ; but do not these writers deserve to be read twice ? Has not the teacher of youth the choice of spending much or little time in his own hand ? "

[1] Herbart, *Science of Education*, p. 91.   [2] Herbart, Ibid., p. 168.

It is to Ziller and Rein that we look for detailed selection and arrangement of studies upon the basis of apperception and a moral revelation of the world through their thought contents.

2. COURSE OF INSTRUCTION

Looking upon the educational procedure in a broad way, Herbart, in the *Science of Education*, distinguishes three methods of procedure; viz. (1) the merely presentative, (2) the analytic, and (3) the synthetic.

1. Only that can be presented according to the first method which is sufficiently similar to that which the pupil has already observed; as, for example, pictures of strange cities, lands, and costumes, with the pictures of other well-known objects; historical descriptions reminding of the present. A mere explication loses in clearness and penetration the further it is removed from the experience of the child. Its rule is, "so to describe that the pupil will imagine that he has a direct sense-perception."

2. Analytic instruction, however, resting on its own strength, has to do more with that which may be separated, that which has reached some degree of universality. That which is simultaneously present can be separated into its parts, and the parts into characteristics. The masses of ideas which course through the mind may be separated, in order to bring clearness to them. Events may also in similar way be separated or analyzed. In all this one comes upon that which *cannot* be separated, which is law-giving for the speculative intellect, and upon that which *should* or *should*

not be separated, which is based upon æsthetic relations, the taste. In analytic instruction we make an
analysis of that which the child knows in a general
way, in order that he may become conscious of that
which is really implied in his knowledge, but not consciously perceived; thus, if we analyze the line, " Art
is long, and time is fleeting," which the student understands well enough in a certain way, we shall discover
a wealth of implied meaning not at first seen. We
may find that " art " means any kind of human activity in which there is productivity — useful arts and
fine arts; that " long " refers to the past and to the
future; that the present status of any art (painting, weaving) is the product of all recorded progress
in the past; that if a man would advance in art, he
must master its past to start with, and manage to get
his advance embodied in some tangible form (a dy-
namo, for instance) ; that, indeed, all machines are the
records of arts that are so " long " that they may
extend over centuries, and that what we call institutions are the spiritual machines of the race; finally,
that all education is the process of making the individual master of these " long " arts. But the advantages of analytical instruction are restricted by the
limitations of that which can be given only in experience. Analysis must take its material as it finds it.

3. Synthetic instruction, however, "which builds
out of its own stones," reaches much farther. It cannot, indeed, be richer than the science and literature
of the world, but it is incomparably richer than the
individual environment of the child. Within its territory lie mathematics and science, together with that

which precedes and follows them, and the whole advance of mankind through the steps of culture from the old to the new. Synthesis has two functions: to give the elements, and to contrive their union. To complete the synthesis is impossible, for this is an unending process.

Herbart now applies the analytic and the synthetic methods of instruction to each of the chief classes of interest. The group of interests arising out of *knowledge* is developed from such subjects as mathematics and natural science, while that arising from human association (*Theilnahme*) comes out of those subjects which relate to man, such as history, literature, and religion. We cannot at present follow him through these applications, though they are highly suggestive to the teacher.

In view of certain developments in the Herbartian school, it will be interesting to note Herbart's attitude toward religion. He says: "The youth is likely to lose himself in opinions. His character must guard him from ever thinking it desirable to have no religion; his taste must be too pure ever to find the discord bearable which necessarily arises in a world without moral order; that is to say, which arises out of a world of realities without the reality of God." He thinks the religious feeling of childhood should be cherished, for it is impossible suddenly to restore a lost religious sensibility through speculative conviction. "Yet positive religion as such does not belong to the school, but to the church and to the parents." The followers of Herbart, seizing upon the fact that Germany is a unit in demanding the teaching of relig-

ion in the schools, have made this the pivot about
which everything turns and to which everything is
related. This may be regarded as purely accidental,
and by no means necessary to a thorough application
of Herbartian principles.

3. Methods of Instruction

Here again Herbart discusses the subject in principle rather than in concrete detail; while the brief
exposition he gave has, in his successors, grown to be
an important chapter, under the general title of the
Formal (or rational) Stages of Instruction (Die formalen Stufen des Unterrichts).[1]

Antecedent to a consideration of the four steps to
be observed as a principle of instruction, we shall need
to examine briefly Herbart's view of *attention* as a
phase of apperception, and his very suggestive distinction between mental *absorption* and rational *reflection.*

We have seen that all mental life consists in the
reciprocal actions, relations, and conditions of the
ideas; that the business of education is to supply
ideas, to assist in their arrangement, and to bring their
proper relations before consciousness. An ideal system of pedagogics must show how this is to be done.
We are indebted to Herbart, perhaps, more than to
any other man, for a series of fine observations giving

---

[1] The following works may be cited at this point: Wiget, *Die
formalen Stufen*; Rein, *Outlines of Pedagogics*, Van Liew's translation, Syracuse, N.Y.: C. W. Bardeen, 1893; DeGarmo, *Essentials
of Method*, Boston: D. C. Heath & Co., 1893; McMurry, *General
Method*, Bloomington, Ill.: Public-School Publishing Co., 1893.

clearness and certainty to the procedure of instruction.

The first step in this direction is the doctrine of Attention, a subject that has received its most exhaustive and fruitful treatment at Herbart's hands.

Voluntary and involuntary attention are the two parts into which the subject naturally falls.

(a) *Voluntary Attention* — This is brought about through the effort of the will in obedience to some remote purpose of the teacher in government or training. In this case the representations are *given* to consciousness and are not spontaneous (*freisteigend*). At this point one of the greatest and commonest mistakes of teachers is made. They imagine that when they are forcing attention or inducing it by means of remote ends, such as good marks, emulation, high rank in school, prizes, etc., that they are best serving the child and the school. They do not consider that they are losing sight of the main purpose, which is the excitation of direct interest. This can arise only out of the subject itself. The voluntary attention, however, is by no means to be rejected in those cases where self-control is necessary, as in long-continued direct perception, in learning by heart, etc. For this latter procedure, Herbart gives a number of practical hints. We should not begin with learning by heart even when this itself is the end to be reached. First must come clearness in single perceptions; then their association. There should be no hurry; the beginning must be slow, especially where great difficulties are to be met. Bodily movements, oral recitation, often in concert, writing, drawing, are all helps which are not to be neglected. Even where the memorized matter is to be always held by the memory, perpetual repetition is a questionable means, for it may easily lead to overpressure. It is preferable to exercise the mind by constant application of the matter in hand to that which actually interests the pupil.

(b) *Involuntary Attention* — Involuntary attention is divided into primitive and apperceiving. In primitive attention the idea arises solely through its own individual power; in apperceiving attention it is assisted or reinforced through its connection with ideas already present. For the primitive attention, Herbart lays down four rules: —

1. The sense-impression must have sufficient strength; hence the need of direct sense-perception of things. This failing, a picture is preferable to a description.

2. Excess of sense-impression must be avoided, so that receptivity may be prolonged.

3. A rapid piling up of one thing upon another must be avoided. There must be singling out, separation, procedure step by step, in order that through the opposition of the ideas a hindrance or mutual arrest shall not arise among them.

4. There must be intermissions, or resting-points, so that the aroused ideas may have time to restore their equilibrium, or, in other words, so that the child may have time enough to apprehend, in its proper connection, what has been given to him. It is not advisable, therefore, to hold young children to recitation for long periods at a time.

The apperceiving attention is that state of the mind

in which each new representation is brought into proper union or relation with those already present. It is of the greatest importance in education, and although presupposing and depending upon the primitive attention, it is observed very early in life. Apperception must constantly be exercised in all instruction, for instruction is given in words only; the ideas upon which the interpretation of the words depends must be supplied by the hearer, or learner. When this kind of attention is once properly pursuing its course, it should not be disturbed. The teaching must go on until it has satisfied the expectation that it has aroused. The solution must plainly answer to the problem. Everything must be connected. Attention is disturbed by untimely pauses or by the introduction of foreign matter. It is disturbed when that is brought into the light which should have remained in shadow. The same is true of oft-repeated words, set forms of expression — everything that emphasizes the language at the expense of the subject-matter; this is true even of rhymes, stanzas of poetry, and rhetorical adornment when used in the wrong place. A fundamental rule is that, before being set at work, the pupil shall be led into a field of consciousness similar to that in which his work is to lie. This can be done at the beginning of a recitation hour by giving a short review of the work of the preceding lesson or by a general review of that which is to be attempted, or by both. This thought is more fully developed by Herbart's disciples. Instruction builds upon the foundation of experience already gained in or out of the school. The fact that that which is already possessed is to be widened and strengthened and arranged, excites attention and expectation. If that which is already possessed is not strong and vivid enough, it must be reproduced in order to lead the pupil into the field of thought where his work lies. The right care for the apperception, *i.e.*, the proper distribution of the masses of ideas as they exist in consciousness or come into it, is of the greatest importance in methodical instruction. For, only by a vital and consistent uniting of new ideas to those already present, can the compass of thought be continually extended and made a permanent acquisition. This is the reason why the teaching of great numbers of unrelated facts, in geography and history, for instance, is such a fatal blunder.

(c) *Mental Absorption and Reflection* — In the activity of the mind in taking on or apprehending the ideas in their manifoldness, we meet with the notions of Absorption (*Vertiefung*) and Reflection (*Besinnung*). Absorption is the giving up of one's self to an object in thought. It is the special care that one gives to a subject in order to apprehend it fully and to enter into it. But absorption should not be distorted. A single, habitual frame of mind that would falsify and minimize all other impressions, must be avoided. "The mind should manifest itself clearly in many directions."

But again, the personality that rests upon unity of consciousness would not obtain in continuous absorption, if the collecting power of reflection did not step in to unite the manifold that absorption has given. Reflection must, however, avoid the synthesis of the contradictory, for where this occurs confusion follows, or the mind is lost in doubt and irrational desires. "But the true significance of reflection (*Besinnung*) is not that what we call inner synthesis, consists merely in a uniting of ideas in general, but that we simultaneously gather them about the focus of our self-consciousness, and make ourselves aware of them as our possessions, or mental states."[1] But since the two notions, absorption and reflection, exclude each other, each must pass over into the other. Herbart calls them the inspiration and expiration of the soul.

It is in this connection that we come next to the logical distinction of four steps, or stages, in instruction and method. They are: (1) clearness; (2) association; (3) system; (4) method.

(d) *The Formal Steps of Instruction* — Taking up the four notions in order, we have: —

1. *Clearness* — By this term Herbart means the apprehension of the individual, or single object as such. The manner of instruction is simple presentation on the part of the teacher and reception on the part of the pupil. It may, according to one of Pestalozzi's methods of elementary instruction, consist in the teacher's presenting a word or a sentence to the class and having the latter repeat the same, singly or in concert. In general, it means the perception of any concrete or individual fact by the pupil. This step is one of absorption.

2. *Association* — This consists in a progress from one absorption to another, as opposed to the non-pro-

---

[1] Schmidt, *Encyclopädie der Pädagogik*, art. "Herbart."

gressive absorption of the first step.   It appears as a
uniting that is determined through the imagination,
"which tastes every compound and rejects only the
tasteless."   Association is not complete when, in that
which is learned, there is not force enough to bring
the imagination to the front, or when that which is
learned checks its action.   The method for this step
is conversation, which gives the pupil an opportunity
to investigate, to change, to make consistent the accidental union of thoughts, and to assimilate, after his
own fashion, what is learned.   This step, although
characterized as absorption, seems to contain elements
of reflection.   It is an elementary stage in the process
of apperception, or assimilation of knowledge.

3. *System* — This is the step in which each part of
that which is learned finds its proper place in relation
to the other parts.   It evidently belongs to the non-
progressive reflection (*ruhende Besinnung*).   It is the
rich arrangement of a rich reflection.   "Its essential
condition is clearness of the individual elements; its
method is the connected discourse.   The bare statement of an all-pervading principle does not suffice to
bring its importance into view, except to him who
reflects.   To see the importance and bearing of this
principle one need only consider what a chaos instruction is when coördination does not come in to unite
and articulate any given manifold."   Just as the mind
synthesizes the manifold of sensation into significant
unities, so the teacher should synthesize the manifold
given in instruction, in order that each factor may
find its place in an organic whole.   This stage com-
pletes the association of the elements of knowledge,

and brings about the highest scientific organization of which the pupil is capable.

4. *Method* — By this term Herbart understands the well-ordered self-activity of the pupil in the solution of tasks, and in investigation under the leadership of the teacher. He sees in this step the progressive reflection. The mode of procedure is to assign tasks and problems whose preparation is the duty of the pupils, and which the teacher corrects.

As before remarked, it is one of the chief merits of the Herbartian school to have further developed these thoughts of the master.[1] We may therefore defer a more minute discussion of the subject, and close this department of our topic with a few quotations of general import.

Herbart says : "In general, absorption should precede reflection, but just how far it should do so remains undetermined. Certainly the two must be kept together as closely as possible, for we wish no absorption that would be harmful to personal unity, the condition of which is reflection. We can desire no reflection whose long and unbroken continuance would create a tension under which a sound mind could not exist in a sound body. In order, therefore, to keep the mind in balance, we prescribe the general rule : give equal prominence to absorption and reflec-

---

[1] The most elaborate application of these four ideas, now known in Germany as the formal stages of instruction, is found in Dr. Rein's *Theorie und Praxis des Volksschulunterrichts nach Herbartischen Grundsätzen*. In these books all the work of the eight school years is laid down in great detail, and a large number of model exercises worked out according to the formal steps. This epoch-making work will be considered in Part II.

tion in every group of objects, even the smallest; that is to say, emphasize equally clearness of the individual perception, association of the manifold, coördination of the associated, and progress through exercise according to this coördination. Upon these conditions depends the charm which should rule in everything that is learned."

In this connection Herbart's protest against tediousness in the school-room is pertinent. He says: " Experience often brings a tediousness that we have to bear, but which the pupil should never have to suffer at the hands of the teacher. *Tediousness is the greatest sin of instruction.* It is the privilege of instruction to fly over steppes and morasses; if it cannot always wander in pleasant valleys, it can at least exercise in mountain climbing and reward with broad fields of view."

CHAPTER VII

SCHOOL DISCIPLINE — GOVERNMENT AND TRAINING

1. GOVERNMENT

THIS chapter is an important one for those who would grasp the whole significance of Herbart's system of education, in which instruction in knowledge, even that apparently non-moral in kind, performs an important function in the development of moral character. At the outset Herbart makes a sharp distinction between mere repressive governmental, or police, regulation, whereby heedlessness, or youthful impetuosity and boisterousness, is held in check without regard to any specific moral effort, and to those more serious, far-reaching efforts that involve the formation of moral habits. By government, then, he means the immediate maintenance of outward order through enforced authority, the holding in check of youthful perversity, partly that education may succeed, partly to secure the safety of the child in many kinds of danger, partly to protect society against childish love of destruction and mischief. Training is moral education itself in so far as it works directly upon the mind. It seeks to build the will, whereas government attempts only to hold it temporarily in restraint. Training is here related and united to instruction, and together with it comprises the whole of education proper. Government works for the present, training for the future. It is the business of government to hold youthful impulses in check until training has time to form a will that shall be able to control them. Great harm ensues when the teacher always governs but never trains; when he imagines that older and shrewder pupils need only shrewder government. The following from Herbart's own words makes perfectly clear the occasion for government, together with its scope and function : —

"The child enters the world without a will of its own, and is therefore incapable of any conscious moral relation. Consequently the parents (partly spontaneously, partly agreeably to the demand of society) can make themselves master of the child as of a chattel. It is true they know well that in the being whom they now, without asking, treat as they like, a Will in the course of time will put itself forth, which they must win over to themselves if the incongruity of a conflict unseemly to both is to be avoided. But it is long before this takes place. At first, instead of a true will, which renders the child capable of determination, there is only a wild impetuosity, impelling it hither and thither, a principle of disorder, disturbing the plans of adults, and placing the future personality of the child itself in manifold dangers. This impetuosity must be *subdued*, or the disorderly character will be put down as the fault of the child's guardians. Subjection is brought about by force, and the force must be sufficiently strong, and often enough repeated, to compass this subjection before any trace of a true will is manifested in the child. The principles of practical philosophy require this.

"But the germs of this blind impulsiveness, these crude desires, remain in the child, and even increase and grow stronger with time. To the end, therefore, that they may not give to the will growing up in their midst an anti-social direction, it is necessary to keep them constantly under an ever-perceptible restraint.

"An adult trained to reason undertakes, as time goes on, to govern himself. There are human beings, however, who never reach this point, and society keeps such under perpetual guardianship, calling some idiots, some prodigals. Some there are who actually cultivate in themselves an anti-social will; with such society is inevitably at war, and generally they are justly worsted in the end. But the conflict is a moral evil for society itself, to prevent which child-government is one among numerous necessary precautions.

"It is obvious that the aim of child-government is manifold — partly avoidance of harm both for others and for the child himself in the present and the future, partly avoidance of strife as an evil in itself, finally avoidance of collision, in which society finds itself forced into a contest for which it is not perfectly authorized.

"It all amounts to this, that such government aims at producing no specific moral result in the mind (*Gemüth*) of the child, but only at creating a spirit of order.   Nevertheless, it will soon be clear that the cultivation of the child-soul cannot be altogether a matter of indifference to government." [1]

These childish offences arise out of desires having a bodily or mental origin.   The wise teacher seeks to remove their cause.   For example, if disturbance arise from physical restlessness, this is an indication that seats are uncomfortable, or that the air is bad, or the temperature too high or too low, or that the recitation periods are too long.   Disturbances arising from mental conditions must likewise be traced to their source, that the disturbing cause may be removed. The impulse to mental activity is one of the strongest in the child.   If school work is not properly planned, some children will receive no food for mental activity from the teacher, and will, of course, supply their own. It follows naturally, when the teacher has been able to excite only indirect or transient interest, such as results from mere government or unworthy incentive to study, that disturbances arising from mental dissatisfaction are always imminent.   In such cases the disturbing cause is the teacher.

The watchful attention of the teacher is a means of government to prevent disorder.   Again, the teacher may demand obedience to his directions.   If the obedience is to follow as a result of the teacher's authority, without inquiry into reasons, then any means taken to secure obedience belong to the department of government.   The obedience that follows the directions of the teacher, because the pupil in consequence of

[1] *Science of Education*, pp. 95, 96.

reflection has agreed to their correctness, falls, not under government, but under training. The means of enforcing commands are warnings, threats, and finally punishments, at' the end of which stands corporal chastisement. Yet more fundamental to government are two ruling, complementary ideas, AUTHORITY and LOVE. Of them Herbart says: "The mind bends to authority; its peculiar movements are constrained by it, and it may thus be of considerable service in suppressing a growing will which tends to perverseness. It can be least dispensed with in the case of the most energetic natures, for these make trial of the bad as well as the good, and pursue the good if they are not lost in the bad. But authority is obtained only through superiority of mind, and this, as is well known, cannot be reduced to rules. It must act independently, without reference to education. A logical and far-reaching course of action once prescribed, must openly and freely take its own straight course, regardful of circumstances, but undisturbed, untroubled by the likes or dislikes of a weaker will. If the careless boy breaks rudely into the prescribed circle, he must be made to feel what he might spoil. If the wanton desire to spoil arises in him, the intention, so far as it becomes or could become an act, must be richly punished; but the teacher must scorn to take any notice of the bad will, together with the insult implied therein. To wound the desire to do evil, which the government of children is as powerless as the state to *punish*, with the deep disapproval it deserves, is the business of education, which begins only after government has done its work. For the way to utilize authority once attained, we must look beyond government to education proper. For though mental culture gains nothing directly from passive obedience to authority, the marking out or enlargement of the circle of thought which depends upon it, and in which the pupil moves freely and builds up himself independently, is of the highest importance.

Love depends on the harmony of the feelings and on habit. The difficulty a stranger finds in winning it at once becomes apparent. He who secludes himself, who speaks much in hard tones, and becomes excited about trifles, will assuredly never gain it; nor, on the other hand, will he who makes himself familiar — who, when he should be kind and yet at the same time maintain his ascendancy, seeks his own pleasure by taking part in the enjoyment of the children. The harmony of feelings that love demands, may arise in two ways. Either the teacher enters into the feelings of the pupil, and without permitting it to be noticed, joins in them with tact, or he takes care that the feelings of the pupil can approach his own in some particular way; this is more difficult, but must, nevertheless, be combined with the other, because only when it is possible for the pupil to unite his activity in some way or other with the teacher's can he contribute force of his own to the relationship between them.

"But a boy's love is transitory and fitful unless sufficient strength of habit be added. Time, tender care, intercourse alone with the individual, strengthen the relationship. We need not say how much this love, once won, lightens the task of government; but it is so important to education proper (since it imparts to the pupil the teacher's bent of mind), that those deserve the severest blame who so readily and so fatally make use of it to gratify themselves by the exhibition of their power over their children."

2. TRAINING, OR DISCIPLINE IN THE LARGE SENSE

To show more fully, however, what relation training, or discipline in the wider sense, bears to the formation of character, Herbart offers the following trenchant remarks upon the attempts that many make to form character through repression or by harping upon the chords of sensibility : —

"Direct action on the youthful mind with a view to habit, is discipline, or training. It appears, then, there is a possibility of forming the character by merely acting on the feelings without reference to the circle of thought. It might indeed appear to be so, if we were wont, without further search, to give ideas logically put together out of properties the credit of reality .

"But it will appear quite otherwise if we interrogate experience. At least, whoever has noticed into what an abyss of pain and misfortune a human being may fall, and even remain for long periods, and yet, after the time of trouble has passed, rise up again apparently almost unchanged, the same person, with the same aim and opinion, even the same manner — whoever, we say, has noticed this, will hardly expect much from that swaying of the emotions, by which mothers especially so often believe they are educat-

ing their children. Besides, when we see what degrees
of paternal strictness a robust youth will endure, and
remain untouched, what incentives are wasted on
weak natures without making them stronger, how
temporary is the whole reaction which follows the
action, we way well advise the educator not to prepare false relations, for himself, which are usually the
only residue of *mere* discipline!

"To me all these experiences are but confirma-
tions of an extremely simple psychological conviction,
namely, that all feelings are but passing modifica-
tions of the existing presentations, and then when the
modifying cause ceases, the circle of thought must
return by itself to its old equilibrium. The only
result I should expect from mere stimulation of the
emotions, would be a fatal blunting of the finer feelings, the place of which would be taken by an artificial sensibility which in the course of years would
but foster pretence with all its troublesome offshoots.

"The case is indeed entirely different, when *the
circle of thought receives additions as opportunity offers,*
or when *endeavors pass into action and thereby become
will.* These conditions must be taken into account in
order to interpret experience correctly.

"At this point, we can judge what discipline may
be to education. All *changes* of feeling the pupil must
suffer, are only necessary transitions to determinations
of the circle of thought, or of character. And thus
the relation of discipline to formation of character is
twofold — indirect and direct. It partly helps to
make that instruction possible which will influence
the subsequent formation of the character of the fu-

ture independent man; it is partly a means even now to create or not to create, through action or inaction, as the case may be, a beginning of character. It is impossible to instruct an ungovernable boy, and the boyish tricks he plays are to be taken in a certain way as indications of his future personality, though, as every one knows, with considerable limitations. An unruly boy acts mostly from fleeting fancies; doubtless he learns thereby what he can do, but the first element necessary to fix the will is here wanting — a firm, deeply-rooted desire. Only where this forms the basis, do boyish tricks help to determine character. The *first* relation of discipline to the formation of character is thus the more important — that, namely, which clears the way for such instruction as will penetrate the thoughts, interests, and desires. Still the second ought not to be neglected, least of all in subjects who are less mobile and act with firmer purpose. The concept of discipline formulated in the beginning is, taken merely in itself, completely empty. The mere intention to form cannot enter into, or directly act on, the mind in such a way as to become a power really able to form. Those who by means of such *an empty discipline show their good intentions*, work, they know not how, on gentle natures through the spectacle they themselves present; their tender, anxious, urgent manner gives the observant boy the idea of the great importance of the thing which an otherwise honored person has so much at heart. Such teachers then need only be careful not to mar this spectacle in other ways, not to stifle respect by passion or pettiness, or, even worse, lay themselves open to the criti-

cism of the child, often as true as it is sharp. Thus
they will be able to accomplish much for impressionable natures, without, however, being for that reason safe from committing greater errors with less
willing ones." [1]

The most important thought in Herbart's pedagogics is that training shall unite with instruction to
form character. But character-building is will-build-
ing. To understand more fully, therefore, how training is to affect the will, we must make a summary of
Herbart's doctrine of the formation of the will as presented in Chapter III. Will arises out of desire when
coupled with a conviction of the possibility of its attainment. The idea in its strength and completion
is will. But along with every action of the will there
is present in consciousness a mass of ideas concerning motives, duties, considerations, etc., all of which
together form a " picture " of the will-action. When
the will a second time has occasion to make a similar
decision, this "picture " of the former action at once
rises into consciousness. If the second decision coincides with the first, the total representation is much
strengthened and vivified. Later repetitions continue
to deepen the impression. If now, upon a later occasion, a desire arises which contradicts and opposes the
decisions already made, there at once begins a mental
strife or struggle between the opposing ideas, the old
and established group, which has been made strong
and vivid by repeated actions of the will, on the one
side, and the new and opposing desire on the other.

[1] *Science of Education*, pp. 229-231.

If the latter idea falls in with the former, the hindrance is removed, union takes place, and mental peace and comfort follow. If, on the contrary, the decision is opposed to previous right ones, the opposition remains, and a mental discomfort ensues, the highest degree of which is called remorse. Out of single acts of will, then, grows the more general will. Every new similar action strengthens the tendency already at hand. The memory of the will, or reproduction of the will — " pictures," becomes important in this consideration. If the reproduction is to be rapid and clear, the representations of which these " pictures " are composed must be intimately and strongly united. This would be the case, for example, when a will-action arises from energetic and thoroughgoing reflection. The latest series of ideas, then, are examined by the apperception, or synthesizing power of the mind, to see if they can be harmonized and united to the former. The result is a judgment on the matter, out of which rises a command or prohibition. When such a judgment is extended so as to include not merely a single case, but a whole class of similar cases, we call it a practical principle of conduct, or maxim. " If these maxims are to hold good for life, they must arise through and out of life; true maxims are always the expression of a portion of the life history of an individual. Maxims which have their origin in the thinking reflection, as, for example, in instruction, must be practised in life to become real maxims." [1] It is the business of training to see that

<hr>

[1] Volkmann, *Lehrbuch der Psychologie*, ii., 454.

all classes of will-action are brought under the dominion of moral maxims, in order that a "symmetrical
passion for good" may be created. "Character is, in
general, uniformity and fixedness of the whole of
will."

Children have at first no real moral character. It
arises gradually, and begins when here and there
single moral volitions arise from the union of similar
acts of will. These more general determinations of
will-action which, through the apperception, begin to
accept or reject the new will-actions, form the beginning of the *subjective side*, or subjective foundations of
character. Over against this stands the *objective part*,
or the single will-act which results from a manifold of
desire. The subjective part of character is *that which
determines;* the objective part is *that which is determined.* In regard to the subjective side of character,
it is the task of instruction, in company with training,
to see to it, not that several lines of thought, existing
alongside of each other, come to validity, "but that
there be secured that unity of a ruling habit of
thought upon which rests the energy and consistency
of will peculiar to character, and through which a
limit is set to the rule of the passions." With these
general remarks about the nature and growth of will,
we may turn to the more individual phases of training.

Empty training, the mere playing upon the chords
of sensibility, is by all means to be avoided, for it
merely deadens feeling without effecting anything
more.

It is the duty of training to care for the deed,

through whose courage the will is strengthened; of course to further the good, to suppress the bad.

There are two characteristics of the will-furthering deed: (1) It must have an aim of real, earnest significance, and (2) it must proceed from an earnest desire of the child; must spring from a direct rather than an indirect interest. It is the business of training not to suppress disorder, but to cultivate that habitual right tone of mind so essential for instruction. It seeks to remove disturbing influences, so that no matters of overpowering temporary interest fill the mind. It seeks to secure a collected state of mind in pupils. It works to the end that the same docility, willingness, and openness be ever present or newly awakened, and if the pupil has reached the point where his self-activity suffices as impelling and guiding force, training seeks to give him the needed quietude. In its direct influence upon the will, training has for its end fixedness or firmness of character.

The factors of its activity are as follows : —

1. It limits and enlivens action according to its own sense. In that it limits, it meets the closely related government, but its "accent" is very different,— not short and sharp, but measured; of slow penetration and gradual withdrawal. It limits harmful action through diverting employment and through punishment. This last, however, belongs to training only when the action is seen to be deliberate, and where new excitations break forth, which, continued, would impress false features upon the mind. It enlivens action where the present tendency of thought gives hope of a correct determination of character.

2. In reference to what has been called the objective side of character, *i.e.*, the volition resulting from a manifold of desire, training must support and determine (*halten und bestimmen*). By the first of these is meant the correct procedure of training in order to effect the memory of the will. This is brought about when the teacher always conducts himself toward the pupil with quiet and fixed certainty, never losing presence of mind, and always answering to the tone of mind in which he has placed his pupils. The teacher must be so won for education that he himself is largely determined by the pupils, and then, through a natural reflex influence, will determine them. The teacher must press the naturally determining feelings so penetratingly upon the pupil that he will early perceive the true relation of things. Here is the place for the punishment which is to train. It is distinguished from the purely police punishment, in that it is not adjusted by any measure of retribution, but must be so measured as always to appear as well-meant warning, which does not excite ill-will toward the teacher. It avoids as much as possible the positive and arbitrary, and limits itself where it can to the natural consequences of human action. Rewards are to be given according to the same principle.

3. In relation to the *subjective* or *determining* side of character, training should be *regulative* and *supporting*. Here the principles of action which the pupils themselves have, are taken into account. Training lets it be felt that it does not understand an inconsequent action. Furthermore, it calls attention to the crudity of hap-hazard principles of conduct, but it never treats

slightingly what springs from earnestness of purpose, even though it may deserve and receive reproof. Training gives support in the struggle of principles to assert themselves, provided, of course, that they deserve support. Here authority and an exact knowledge of the pupil's mind are important. "For it is precisely the inner authority of the child's own principles of action which must be supplemented and strengthened by an external but exactly similar authority."

This in general is the application of training to the work of education. Herbart adds some important remarks, however, in reference to morality. The memory of the will is not always desirable, for the bad may be remembered as well as the good. Training must seek to put to confusion and shame that which is evil. The estimate of the good-will is not to be determined by the result of the action. In early youth, when instruction and environment invite to the first apprehension of moral truth, Herbart demands the preservation of a quiet, clear frame of mind, and the preservation of a child-like sense. That is harmful which opposes a natural forgetfulness of self. Just as the healthy body is not felt, so the care-free child does not feel its existence, for it should not make itself the measure of the importance of that which is external to itself. All, then, which continuously and actively calls attention to self is harmful for moral training. These disturbances may arise from pain, pleasure, sickness, and exciting temperature, bad treatment, frequent teasing, neglect of needful care, or from anything which feeds vanity and self-love. Further, in this period the tender feelings of the child must be protected and favored by the removal of everything which can accustom the imagination to the morally hateful. This excessive care would with growing years and moral power be a mistake, for in the moral as in the physical world, long-continued tenderness is a poor means of protection against rigor of climate. It is only with the negligent educator that the child takes up and imitates all he sees. The making glad through deserved approval is the fine art of training.

Part II

EXTENSION AND APPLICATION OF HERBART'S
EDUCATIONAL IDEAS IN GERMANY

CHAPTER I

TUISKON ZILLER AND KARL VOLKMAR STOY

The Two Schools

THESE two men are the pioneers in the application of Herbart's theories to the work of the schools. Herbart himself, whose teaching experience was confined to tutoring, a form of education that seems always to have hovered before his mind, had little opportunity in his university career to put his system into actual operation in the school-room. This was left to his successors.

Born about the same time and coming alike under the influence of Herbart, both Ziller and Stoy began earnestly to reduce his theories to practice. Each became the representative of a specific interpretation of the doctrines. In this way two schools arose. The Stoy school held to Herbart's theory mostly in its original form, making their chief work the application of it to the various elementary and secondary schools. Dr. Stoy himself gave most attention to the working out of the system in the elementary schools, while his most renowned coadjutor, Dr. Otto Frick, late Director of the great Orphan School, or *Frankesche*

101

GEN. THEO. SEMINARY
LIBRARY

Stiftungen, established by Francke in Halle, did a monumental work in applying it to the secondary schools, or gymnasiums.

Professor Ziller, on the other hand, struck out more independently, giving a wider and freer interpretation to Herbart's ideas. He applied Herbart's principles for the selection of the subject-matter of instruction with a freedom that caused the more conservative to gasp with dismay. Not content with one master-stroke, he made another equally startling to orthodox educators, by proposing in all seriousness a remarkable method of articulating, coördinating and unifying instruction. This is known as his theory of CON-CENTRATION, an exposition of which will be found in the chapters on Ziller, and his most aggressive follower, Dr. William Rein, of Jena.

We may now turn to a detailed study of the leaders of the two schools, treating first Ziller and his followers, then Stoy and his adherents, it being understood that in some cases the classification is a loose one.

GEN THEO SEMINARY
LIBRARY

CHAPTER II

TUISKON ZILLER

1. LIFE AND WORKS

ZILLER was born on the 22d of December, 1817, at Wasungen, a village in Saxe-Meiningen. He first attended the gymnasium in Meiningen, and afterwards studied philology in the University of Leipsic. He then became a teacher in the gymnasium where he had once sat as a pupil. In 1853, however, he returned to Leipsic to qualify as *privat docent* in law. But his teaching experience in Meiningen had given him a fondness for educational questions, and in 1856 he published his first pedagogical essay, *Introduction to General Pedagogy.*[1] In the following year he issued his treatise on *The Government of Children,*[2] which is an extension and application of Herbart's idea, already described. These works soon attracted public attention. With the assistance of Dr. C. Barth, he now founded in connection with the university at Leipsic a pedagogical seminary and practice school, modelled after that of Herbart at Königsberg. This

[1] *Einleitung in die allgemeine Pädagogik.*
[2] *Die Regierung der Kinder.*

seminary ceased to exist upon the death of its founder in 1883.

In was in 1865 that Ziller's epoch-making work, *Basis of the Doctrine of Instruction as a Moral Force*,[1] appeared. By many this book was looked upon as a stroke of genius. At any rate it marks the beginning of popular interest in the philosopher Herbart, who in his lifetime, though occupying prominent positions, had been thrown into the background by the more dazzling philosophical systems of idealism founded by Kant, Fichte, Schelling, and Hegel. As an index of the newly awakened interest, the Herbart Association, under the title, *Verein für Wissenschaftliche Pädagogik*, was founded in 1868, with Professor Ziller at its head. The *Verein* has since spread all over Germany, and numbers many hundreds of adherents. It is, for the most part, broken up into local clubs for the study of educational problems from the Herbartian standpoint. *Lectures on General Pedagogy*,[2] a text-book on educational theory, appeared in 1876; and in 1881, Ziller's last work, *General Philosophical Ethics*,[3] was published. He died in 1883 at the age of sixty-six years, having been for a long time a sufferer from severe physical ailments.

2. Ziller's Interpretation of Herbart

Whatever may be thought of the ultimate outcome of Ziller's work, it deserves respect as the most thor-

[1] *Grundlegung zur Lehre vom erziehenden Unterricht.*
[2] *Vorlesungen über allgemeine Pädagogik.*
[3] *Allgemeine philosophische Ethik.*

oughgoing attempt ever made to answer the question, How may instruction in the common school become an instrument for the development of moral character?, It can scarcely be denied that Ziller is thoroughly Herbartian in his foundations. He asks three questions as follows: —

1. What must be selected from human knowledge as the subject-matter of instruction?

2. How must these studies be coördinated so as to conduce to the most perfect mastery of knowledge, the clearest insight into moral relations, and the formation of the highest moral ideals, the best moral disposition, the best moral habits?

3. What method of teaching will best further the above-named ends?

About the investigation of these three subjects one may, with unimportant exceptions, group all that Ziller wrote. His guiding principles, taken directly from Herbart, were as follows: —

1. The conception of moral training through instruction in the common-school branches, keeping the five moral ideas in close touch with the content of the various studies.

2. The apperception of children, or their natural thought-processes founded upon acquired knowledge and social experience, as the only reliable guide to the selection and arrangement of studies, together with the best methods of teaching them.

3. The necessity of developing in the pupils an inherent, far-reaching, and abiding interest in study as a moral revelation of the world.

These are the basal ideas from which he proceeds

and to which he ever returns.   Through the 524 pages
of the *Grundlegung* and the 428 of the *Allgemeine
Pädagogik*, aside from a few incidentals, he labors at
the solution of the three problems from the standpoint of the three fundamental ideas.

The contents of the *Grundlegung* are as follows: —

(*a*) The Relation of Instruction to Government and (moral)
Training.
   § 1.   Government and Instruction.
   § 2.   Two Kinds of Instruction.
   § 3.   Social and Religious Associations in their Relation to
Instruction.
   § 4.   The School as a Place for Moral Training.
   § 5.   The Compass of Instruction.
   § 6.   Relation of Instruction to Moral Training in General.
   § 7.   The Art of Instruction.
        etc., etc., etc.
   (*b*) Specific Ends of Instruction.
   § 12 & § 13.   Interest and Desire.
   § 14.   Direct in Relation to Indirect Interest and to Love.
   § 15.   Many-sided Interest as a Protection against Passionate Desire.
   § 16.   As an Aid to Occupation.
   § 17.   As a Means of Rescue against the Storms of Fate.
   § 18.   As a Means of Perfection.
   § 19.   As related to Personality.
   § 20.   As related to Individuality.

The importance of each of the three lines of investigation regarding the choice, arrangement, and treatment of the various studies warrants a presentation
in separate chapters.

CHAPTER III

ZILLER'S THEORY OF THE HISTORICAL STAGES OF CULTURE

WITHOUT considering in detail the contents of the separate chapters of the *Grundlegung*, we may proceed at once to his treatment of the first of the three great questions of teaching: —

1. What shall be the subject-matter?
2. How shall it be articulated?
3. What shall be the method of instruction?

Taking up the first of these topics, Ziller begins by classifying the school studies into two groups, those that pertain to man, and those that pertain to nature. The humanistic group comprises (1) history, sacred and profane, (2) literature, (3) art, as drawing and music, (4) languages, native and foreign. The group of nature studies consists of (1) geography, (2) natural history, physics and chemistry, (3) arithmetic, (4) geometry, (5) practical exercises, and (6) gymnastics.

Ignoring for the time being the nature studies, Ziller seeks a principle of selection and development for the humanistic, or culture branches.

The first factor in the problem appears to be the fact that we have to do with a developing mind. In no two years of his life are the knowledge, apprehending power, ruling interests, or educational needs of the child the same. He goes somewhat rapidly through a succession of epochs in his mental development. It is not sufficient to demonstrate merely that the child passes through a succession of stages in his mental unfolding; we must have some idea of the nature of the development he goes through if we are to succeed in finding the best possible adjustment of subject-matter to these stages. The current conception of this matter is that it is the faculties that unfold in succession, — perception, then imagination, then memory, then reason, etc., — so that our American pedagogy, in so far as it has any doctrine at all upon the subject, teaches us in a general way to follow this order in the presentation of topics. It is conceivable, further, that the stages of the child's development follow the natural unfolding of the subjects of study according to some logical principle, as, for instance, the order of evolution in biological sciences, or that of increase in complexity of numerical relations, as in mathematics. Were this the case, the key to the presentation of studies would be the most logical unfolding of the various studies as relatively completed sciences. This view, however, meets with serious difficulties. The philosophic order of complete systems may not correspond to the natural psychological order of learning, especially with children. What naturalist, for instance, wishing to give a child a knowledge of nature and love for the study, would begin with a

microscopic investigation of undifferentiated proto-
plasm, or monera of scarcely distinguishable forms?
Nothing in the child's former experience, interest, or
knowledge would throw a particle of light on the subject. Would he not, rather, begin with the familiar
animals of field and forest? The child's development is at all events psychological, and it is plain
that the logical order of developed sciences is not
parallel with it. We must, therefore, look further for
the true principle of apperception in the mind of the
growing child.

The thought over which Ziller most loved to linger,
and for which he cites a host of witnesses, is the somewhat poetic idea, which certainly has biological analogy, that each child in his development from infancy
to manhood passes through the same general stages
that the race has passed through in its rise from
savagery to civilization. This is the argument: Just
as the embryo of one of the higher animals shows
unmistakable evidence of passing through all the essential stages of development manifested by lower
orders, so the child in his mental evolution passes
through, in little, all the great culture epochs that
have marked the development of the race. This is
Ziller's famous doctrine of the historical stages of
culture. If, therefore, one would appeal to the understanding of the child, or touch the springs of his interest, or portray to him ethical relations capable of
claiming his attention, one should be mindful of these
epochs. We are fond of thinking of education as the
process of realizing in each individual the experience
of the race, but we have not emphasized the idea that

the child can best get this experience in the same
order that the race obtained it.

The following from Dr. Rein's *Outlines of Pedagogics*[1]
gives a clear view of the matter as conceived by the
Ziller school. "These considerations turn us back
from the complicated relations of the present, which
are more difficult to grasp, to past times, which are
more simple, more easily understood, and, at the same
time, more easily adaptable to the conceptive power of
the young mind. From this standpoint the material
for the instruction that is to mould character should be
sought in *the development of the national culture*, which
is to be followed in its chief epochs. It should be
presented from its very beginnings, *i.e.*, from the point
at which a constant progress is apparent, up to the
present. This idea, which, agreeably to its content,
we may call the principle of *historical culture*, also
harmonizes, as we shall see at once, with the psychological requirement that the subject-matter in each
case correspond to the child's stage of apperception.
The material and the formal points of view coincide.
A people does not rise at once to a definite height of
culture; centuries of zealous, universal labor are necessary before the height can be reached. It must climb
from lower to ever higher stages; must pass from
simpler to ever more complicated relations in order
to satisfy the bent for improvement and the realization of the kingdom of God upon earth. And the
individual, the same as the people, rises in his development from lower to ever higher stages, from

[1] Syracuse, N. Y.: C. W. Bardeen, 1893.

simpler to ever richer mental contents, if only his ideal tendency be not smothered by material sensuality or by the feeling that he has already attained a fine height. Thus we must accept on the one hand *historical*, on the other hand *individual*, stages of development, or apperception. It is obvious that if the two series — the historical, with its various cultural materials; and the personal, with its manifold ideas, wishes, and desires — can be brought successfully and accurately into harmony with each other, one can undoubtedly get control of the scholar's interest, because by this means the psychological conditions would be best established. The development of the *individual* is nourished on the development of the *whole*. Whenever a subject can claim the height of interest, it enters into the thoughts of the child; being expected, it is welcome, and the direct interest makes its appearance provided the teacher possess the necessary art of instruction. As a matter of course, the most careful selection of material is useless when there is a lack of skill. But this careful selection of subject-matter will give the teacher unsuspected assistance as soon as he understands it.

" We find that this idea of the analogy between the individual and general development of humanity is a common possession of the best and most noted intellects. It appears, for example, in the works of the literary heroes Lessing, Herder, Goethe, and Schiller; with the philosophers Kant, Fichte, Schelling, Hegel, Comte; with the theologians Clement of Alexandria, Augustine, Schleiermacher; with the Darwinists Huxley and Spencer; with the classical philologists F. A.

Wolf, Niethammer, Dissen, Lübker; with the educators Rousseau, Pestalozzi, Froebel, Diesterweg, Herbart, Ziller, and others.

"From the large number of voices let us select but two, Goethe and Kant. The former said : 'Although the world in general advances, the youth must always start again from the beginning, and, as an individual, traverse the epochs of the world's culture.' The latter points out that the education of the individual should imitate the culture of mankind in general, as developed in its various generations." [1]

If, therefore, we are to regard this principle as substantially true, if there is in reality such a parallelism between the successive stages of the child's mental growth and the culture epochs of the race as this theory claims, then, as Ziller and Rein declare, a striking advantage at once comes to view, the psychological principle coincides with the historical one of the material of study, so that without further search we have a common guide to the development of the several culture branches.

What shall be done with the nature-studies is another story, which can be told only when we consider the subject of correlation, or CONCENTRATION, as Ziller calls it.

This idea of the culture-stages was foreshadowed by Herbart when he insisted that Greek should come before Latin because it corresponds more closely to the child's comprehension and interest, also when he said : "Periods which no master has described, whose spirit no poet breathes, are of little value to education." [2]

---

[1] *Outlines of Pedagogics*, pp. 96–98.

[2] Herbart's *Science of Education*, p. 74.

CHAPTER IV

ZILLER'S THEORY OF CONCENTRATION OF STUDIES

THE progress of the thought will now be best com-
prehended by taking up the second grand topic: —
WHAT PRINCIPLE SHALL GOVERN THE ARTICULATION,
OR COÖRDINATION OF THE VARIOUS STUDIES?

Why, first of all, should we strive for any coördination of studies? Chiefly for three reasons, say the
Herbartians, two psychological and one ethical.

1. Instead of regarding the self, or "I," as an
empty point of personality, the same whether rich or
barren in experience, whether ignorant or learned, we
may think of the self, or *ego*, as a constantly growing,
developing somewhat, whose true unity, or individuality, depends upon the unity that exists in its knowledge and experience in general. Abstracting the
content of my mental life, I am *I* only in the sense
that an unrealized possibility is equal to nothing else;
but not abstracting from what I know and feel and
do, I am *I* to the extent that conscious unity exists
among the various elements of my mental life. If
my ideas cannot be related when they pertain to
related things, to this extent I fail to realize my true
being. One of the forms of insanity is plurality of

113

mental existence. But this unity depends upon proper correlation of ideas. The elements in the content of our mental life must be so organized that unity of knowledge and consistency of feeling and volition may arise. Our interests grow out of our knowledge; our feelings, desires, and motives are the natural consequence of our interests; our wills strive to realize the good to self revealed by motives based on knowledge. Symmetrical character is hardly conceivable aside from symmetrical, coördinated knowledge. A man may indeed rule powerfully within a small range of concepts of which he is master, but put him into situations that he does not understand, and his customary strength becomes weakness. Much of a proper correlation of knowledge comes to us spontaneously in spite of teacher or text-book, yet it is easily conceivable that a proper progress in the sequence of topics in each subject, together with a happy juxtaposition of the related parts of all subjects, might aid materially in bringing our knowledge into a substantial unity. If each subject is to be an errant comet, pursuing its path independent of the others — if, in other words, disorganization and isolation of topics is to rule in our instruction — it is plain that the desirable unity of knowledge will not only not be promoted, but will actually be hindered; that consequently the teacher, in spite of his pious wish for the highest welfare of the pupil, may aid in making him a dependent being, whose unrelated knowledge does him little or no good. Our desire to develop the individuality and power of the pupil can find its best realization, so far as instruction is concerned, in the best possible coördination of all the subjects that we teach. The first purpose of the coördination of studies is, therefore, the promotion of true unity and consistency in our mental life through instruction.

2. In the next place, knowledge gained at school may mean much or little for our subsequent careers. According to the formal-culture idea, the result of the training is largely independent of knowledge retained or interests awakened. If the urchin only "buckles to" and learns his lesson, he may forget it as soon as he likes : the advantage is still his, for he has had the discipline. There is, however, another way of looking at these matters, and that is this : if the lad remembers little of what he learns ; if having learned to read, he cares little for useful reading ; if having been forced to acquire a certain mass of knowledge, no permanent effect remains upon his interests, tastes, or pursuits, then this formal training upon which we pride ourselves is practically worthless. It would have been better to let the boy pursue those occupations in which he had some interest, for only where there is interest in things learned can profit result. This is Ziller's view. Now, the coördination of studies means their correlation ; that is, it means that it shall enable the pupil in one way or another to become conscious of useful and interesting relations among the various topics of the various studies. Every child is sure to be interested in something, so that if he can see that other things are related to his favorite ones, life at once broadens before him. This basis of interest in study is laid when the child finds in the subject-matter of instruction that which appeals

to his own thinking as valuable. He must understand it, therefore, primarily, in its relation to himself. The richer the content in his eyes, the more
varied and intimate the relations that are revealed to
him, the warmer is his interest, the more willingly
he pursues study for its value in promoting the things
of which he is most fond. Is it not plain, therefore,
that the more knowledge is knit together, the more
light one subject throws upon another, the richer
will be his apprehension and the warmer his interest?
For the reason, consequently, that coördination of
studies promises to increase rapidly the pupil's power
of apprehension and to promote his direct interest
in what the school has to offer him, it seems worth
working for.

3. It has been stated that there is one ethical reason for the coördination of studies. This, too, is an
outcome of the new way of looking at psychology. A
favorite notion with Germans, and perhaps with all
Christian people, is that the school ought to develop
the moral and religious character of pupils. The old
way took but little note of the studies of the school
as implements for this training, but relied mainly on
authority, first of the Scriptures, and then of teachers,
parents, etc. This is the natural outcome of a psychological system of independent "faculties." But Ziller's
view of which I am writing, not underestimating the
value of the old training, adds, as we have often seen,
the important thought that the common school studies
themselves may become no mean instruments for ethical culture. This idea is a natural outcome of the
notion that interests, desires, and motives are formed

in consequence of ideas gained through study and observation, and that consequently the will itself is
directly dependent upon ideas, or knowledge, for its
field of activity. To bring about unity or consistency
in our volitional acts, therefore, it would seem that
the body of knowledge in which volition has its roots
should be unified to the greatest practicable extent.
If knowledge lies in isolated tracts, it has in the first
place little cumulative effect upon the motives of the
child; and in the second place, even if each separate
tract should give rise to its own little round of interests and motives, there is small probability that the
resulting acts of will would of themselves drop into a
coördinated line of consistent actions. Dr. Rein sums
the matter up as follows: "The ethical need demands
that the teacher shall endeavor to concentrate the
spiritual forces of the pupil, so that they shall not be
dissipated, but shall in their union call forth strong,
effective action. Without such concentration of mental forces no moral character is conceivable. But if the
pupil is to be able to effect this concentration of his
powers, the greatest care must be taken that his mental store be not broken up into disconnected parts, but
unified to the greatest possible extent."

There is, in addition to these theoretical grounds, a
practical reason for the proper coördination of studies,
that should cause us to listen to all serious propositions looking to that end. It is universally acknowledged that our present curriculum, if not already badly
congested, is likely soon to become so. Subject after
subject has been added, not from any demonstrated
pedagogical need, but in obedience to popular demands

or to the professional zeal of specialists. The process
is still continuing. Not only each newly-developed
branch of useful knowledge, but even every popular
social reform (scientific temperance, for instance) demands a representation in the school-room. The result
is often a detrimental atomization of the pupil's time
and attention. Not having time to digest any subject
thoroughly, he soon becomes a mere taster in all learning. The initial stages of our educational progress
were brought about by men like Comenius and Pestalozzi, who were impelled more by their sympathies and
instincts than by clear, analytical thinking; it would
seem that we are still following our instincts to put
into the school everything good in itself, but that we
are taking little heed of the effect upon the child.
Nothing appears more essential to our further advance,
therefore, than a rigid examination of the curriculum,
that indispensable parts may be properly related and
needless ones eliminated.

Some of the reasons why coördination of studies is
desirable having been examined briefly, the interesting
question now arises, How is the coördination to be
effected? Ziller's plan is one of concentration about
a core of culture material. This core about which the
work of each successive grade is to be concentrated is
to be composed of the studies that have the greatest
moral content, or practical value in bringing about the
moral revelation of the world in the mind of the child.
They constitute the material that serves best to cultivate ideals and disposition, being called, indeed, *Gesinnungs-Stoff*.[1] History and literature naturally consti-

[1] That is, material that serves to cultivate right disposition.

tute the core of concentration, the one narrating the actual progress of the race, the other picturing ethical conflict in imaginative forms. Both are concrete, allowing direct access to the ideas they portray, whereas languages have a bar of grammatical and other forms separating the student from the ideas.

Taking advantage of the fact that Biblical history is everywhere taught in German schools, Ziller elaborated a double historical course for them, the one Jewish, the other German. His only serious attempt to utilize literature proper, as a factor of this course, is found in the early years, where he selects twelve of Grimm's fairy tales for the first grade, and Robinson Crusoe for the second. The followers of Ziller still adhere somewhat rigidly to his selections. Later, the Niebelungen Lieder and some of the Thüringer Sagen are used, but after this, not much attention is paid to literature as such. In the double historical series, effort is made to adjust the work for each year to the corresponding epochs in Jewish and German history. The following is the order of topics: First year, Grimm's Fairy Tales; second year, Robinson Crusoe; third year, (1) Bible Stories from the Time of the Patriarchs, (2) Legends of Thuringia (Thüringer Sagen); fourth year, (1) Bible Stories from the Time of the Judges, then of the Kings, (2) Niebelungen Tales; fifth year, (1) Bible Stories from the Time of Christ, (2) History of Henry I., Otto I., Charlemagne; sixth year, (1) Bible Stories from the Time of Christ, continued, (2) Migration of the Nations, Roman Empire and the Popes, the Crusades, the Middle Ages, Rudolph von Hapsburg; seventh year, (1)

The Original Congregations of Churches, and the Apostle Paul, (2) Discovery of America and its First Settlement, History of the Reformation, the Thirty Years' War; eighth year, (1) Instruction in the Catechism, (2) Frederic the Great, the Napoleonic Wars for Independence, the Restoration of the German Empire.

Having decided what the core of concentration shall be, Ziller has now to show how the remainder of the instruction can be grouped about the topics in the leading studies from grade to grade. In the first place, how shall the languages be disposed of? If human deeds, both real and ideal, must of necessity be the expression of the ethical forces at work in the world, it is clear that language is essential for their preservation and transmission. In language, therefore, we find the embodiment of the ethical, so that language study is merely the formal aspect of this culture side of the curriculum. It ought consequently to lend itself, at least to some extent, to the same principle of development. Language being only the vehicle of thought, may naturally be made to follow the development of thought. In this case language would have to be studied as a means for the expression and comprehension of thought, not as an end in itself. Except for minor culture subjects, like drawing and singing, this, for the present, disposes of the first or humanistic group, so far as the principle of concentration is concerned. For a detailed program arranged in harmony with this idea, we must wait for the man who now wears Ziller's mantle, Dr. Wilhelm Rein, Professor of Pedagogy at the University of Jena.

We come now to what may prove the Achilles tendon of Ziller's system. At all events, it is the most critical point — *What shall be done with the nature-studies?*

Having confessedly no moral content, they can at best be used only as *instruments* for moral training. Yet they must be concentrated about the historical epochs of culture. The performance of this task, though seemingly artificial, is not impossible. The second group constitutes geography, nature-studies, and mathematics. The difficulty now with concentration is, not only that nature-studies have no moral content related to the core of concentration, but also that they have no useful historical principle of development. These are difficulties to the Ziller school, yet not insurmountable obstacles.

The path of the progress of science has been that which leads out of darkness into light, from error to truth. Who would, for instance, seriously teach alchemy before chemistry, or astrology before astronomy? We are fond, indeed, of telling our pupils about these beginnings of science, but we speak of them rather as items of interesting information than as necessary to an understanding of science as it exists to-day.

Something can be done, however, in the way of practical concentration. If, as was seen above, the logical order of science as a relatively completed system of knowledge is not a safe guide to its presentation, we may fall back on the psychological principle of apperception, and present it in any way that will appeal to the child's interest and understanding.

It has long been a favorite idea with teachers that geography should be correlated with history. Not only must history have a place in which to unfold, but the unfolding itself has to a large extent been dependent upon the geographical features of the country — its mountains, plains, rivers, seacoasts, forests, and climate. Geography as a basis for history is now becoming an important subject of study in German Universities. It may be added also that it is of much importance in the biological sciences. Thus one might study the Alps as a seat of history, at the same time devoting a part of his attention to Alpine flora and fauna. In a sense, then, geography forms a link to bind together the deeds of man and the facts of nature. In a still larger sense, geography unites nature and man. In these modern times, commerce binds the whole world together. A man in the Northwest may exchange his wheat for the product of any land under the sun. He contributes to the world what he raises, and the world stands ready to give him something of everything in return.

It is geography that first makes the child conscious of the reciprocity that exists in the world, for it shows him in a concrete way, through a study of productions, populations, transportation, and the like, how each man, by the division of labor, works for all men, and is in turn served by all men to the extent of the value of his own contribution.

Geography, then, connects history and science, also revealing the most concrete modes of human reciprocity. It is, therefore, the natural link binding purely humanistic and purely scientific studies. Following this hint, Ziller does not find it difficult to discover some sort of connection between the leading and the subordinate subjects. Dr. Rein calls attention to the fact that the will puts itself into relation to nature in order to bring it into the service of man; that human action is limited by moral rules and by the nature of things. Obedience to moral ideals limits the will as to ends, while obedience to the nature of things limits the will as to means. The ends for which men work, and the means whereby they do it, should be brought to the mind simultaneously.

Finally, mathematics bears the same relation to science that language does to the humanistic studies. It is their formal side. If its real function is made apparent, and its application sufficiently concrete, enough correlation can be brought about to hold the pupil's interest for number and to enhance his interest in that which number measures.

That the Anglo-Saxon teacher who may be curious to know how this arrangement of culture- and nature-studies would look in English, may be gratified, the following outline of single coördinated groups is inserted. It is from the pen of Dr. Frank McMurry, formerly Professor of Pedagogy in the University of Illinois.

FIRST GRADE

Literature: The Fir Tree, Andersen.

Science: (*a*) White Pine as a type of evergreens, since it is more common here than any other evergreen tree.

(*b*) Austrian Pine.

(*c*) Scotch Pine.

(*d*) Norway Spruce.

(*e*) Balsam Fir.

Reading: " A Pine Twig" and "Story of a Pine Tree," in Nature Stories for Young Readers. Also sentences on the board taken from the Science and Literature work, like those immediately following : —

Written Language: Sentences based on Literature, thus : — The fir tree lived in the forest.

It was not happy.

It wished to be tall.

A little rabbit sometimes jumped over the tree.

This made the tree ashamed.

Or based on Science, thus : —

The fir tree is green all winter.

Sometimes the snow covers it.

Then it is a white tree.

The snow does not break the limbs. They bend down.

See how they are fastened into the trunk.

I cannot break off the twigs.

Writing : (All the small letters this year.)

If the children are ready to study *r*, take the words *fir, rabbit, green, tree.*

If some other letter should be studied, similar groups of words bearing on the study of the fir will suggest themselves to the teacher.

Drawing : (*a*) Drawing of pines and firs, with colored chalk or crayon.

(*b*) Drawing, and sewing in perforated board, of evergreen trees, of cones, and of rabbit.

(*c*) Moulding — trunk of evergreen, tub in which it was placed, toys that adorned it.

(*d*) Drawing of different scenes in the story, as of wood-cutters hauling the trees from the forest, etc.

(*a*, *b*, *c*, are from Science, *d* is from Literature.)

Number : Number of needles in a bundle of White, Scotch, or Austrian pine ; in two bundles of White pine ; in two, four, five of Scotch or Austrian pine.

Number of wings on two, three, etc., seeds.

Number of pairs of legs on rabbit.

Number of wheels on wagon that hauled the tree away.
How many span of horses?
Music: "High in the Top of an old Pine Tree."
Poems: "Pine Needles."
"The Little Fir Trees."
"The Pine Tree's Secret."

SECOND GRADE

Literature: "Louise, the Child of the Western Forest," in Seven Little Sisters.

Science: The squirrel (the animal that Louise loved to watch). The quails (of which a beautiful description is given). If squirrels cannot be secured, or are not familiar, the rabbit may first be taken as a type; then the squirrel by comparison. So also with the quail, the hen may first be studied as a type form.

Reading: "The Little Chickens," and "The Chicken Hen," in Easy Steps for Little Feet. "The Squirrel," in Parker's Second Supplementary Reader. "Story of Chicken Little," and "Two Naughty Chickens," in Stickney's Second Reader.

"The Rabbit's Party," in Interstate Second Reader.

"Rover and the Squirrel," in Barnes's Second Reader.

"What the Squirrel Said," in McGuffey's Alternate Supplementary Reader.

Written Language: Stories written by the children about Louise, and also about the animals studied.

Writing: If the children are ready to take up capital L, they will write Louise; if it is C, they will write Christian (Louise's brother) and Christmas (the gala day for them).

Many other capitals can be introduced from the story, and short sentences, or phrases be written, as Little Gretchen, The beautiful river Rhine, Louis loves Fritz.

Drawing: (a) Illustrations of scenes in the story drawn on blackboard or on paper.

(b) Drawing of rabbit, squirrel, hen, and quail; of the ship (on which Louise sailed).

(c) Moulding — log houses, Christian's flute, the axe with

which the father felled the trees, the linen chests (their only furniture), the vegetables (that they raised to sell).

(d) Paper-cutting ; quails, squirrels, vegetables, etc.

Number : (a) How many baby quails has a mother quail ?

Various stories derived therefrom, or if they were to go in couples, how many couples would follow the mother ?

(b) Examples based on the nuts that the squirrels used, measures, pint, quart, etc.

(c) On the number of eggs, how many dozen ?

(d) On the number of logs it takes to build one side of a house.

(e) On the number of dollars Fritz received for a load of wood ; for three or four or five loads.

(f) Children measure and sell vegetables (going with Christian to market).

Song : "Bob White."

"Little Gay Bunny Goat."

"The Queer Little House."

Game : "Hop Little Rabbit" (small chickens represented).

Poems : "Wanted, Twelve Pairs of Stockings."

"The Mountain and the Squirrel."

"Old Squirrel Gray."

THIRD GRADE

Literature : Robinson Crusoe — "Robinson's Harvest."

Science : Wheat — following it from time of sowing until it is taken from the oven as a loaf of bread.

Reading : "The Mill Wheel," in Easy Steps for Little Feet.

"How the Mill Wheel was Turned," Harper's Third Reader.

"What Comes from Seeds."

The Miller's Methods," "The Staff of Life," "The Machine Baker," Information Reader, I.

Written Language : Chapter on Robinson's harvest reproduced in writing. Story of a tiny grain — following a grain of wheat as indicated in the Science lesson.

Writing : Based on sentences taken from the above.

Drawing : (a) Picturing of Robinson, showing his field of grain, his harvest.

(*b*) Drawing a stalk of wheat, a sheaf of wheat: a saber used as a scythe ; pestle and mortar used in pounding wheat ; baskets in which it was held ; clay dish on which it was placed after being fashioned into loaves ; the loaf itself.

(*c*) Moulding of saber, pestle, mortar, basket, plate, and loaf.

(*d*) Paper-cutting ; saber, basket, mortar, pestle.

Number : (*a*) Measure stalks of wheat.

(*b*) Measure wheat by peck, one-half bushel, and bushel. Examples like the following : If I have a bushel, a half-bushel, and a peck of wheat, how many pecks have I ?

(*c*) Weighing a bushel of wheat. How much does a half-bushel weigh ? A peck ? A quart ?

(*d*) Selling wheat at various reasonable prices — the work not to be beyond the pupils.

(*e*) How many grains in a head of wheat ? (choose a head within their possibilities) measure grains in a one-half gill cup. How many such heads will it take to fill it ? To fill a gill cup ?

(*f*) How many bushels can a steam thresher thresh in one day ? In one-half day ? In one hour ?

(*g*) How many bushels of wheat can the Bloomington mill grind in one day ? In a half a day ? etc.

(*h*) What part of a bushel of wheat becomes fine flour ?

(*i*) How many pounds in a sack of flour ? A half-sack ? How many pounds in a sack of graham flour ? In two sacks ?

(*j*) How much does one sack of flour cost ? A half-sack ? Two sacks ? etc.

Songs : " We of the Farmer now will Sing."

" When the Corn begins to Sprout."

Poems : " There was a Jolly Miller."

FOURTH GRADE

History : Fremont's Expedition.

Geography : The country to which the class is introduced through the history, *i.e.*, St. Louis, Mississippi River, Platte River, prairies of Kansas and Nebraska, animals, plants, and products of these states, Fort Laramie, Rocky Mountains in the region of Fremont's Peak, mountains, lakes, etc.; wheat farms, cattle ranches, new Western cities, railroads, frontier facts, garrisons, Indian tribes, prairie fires, blizzards.

Science : The wheat plant, grasses of the West, rocks, fishes, birds, deer, buffalo, etc. If these animals are not all at hand, those most nearly related to them may be studied instead ; for example, the sheep in place of the deer. Also instruments used by Fremont, *i.e.,* the barometer, thermometer, compass (air-pressure and pneumatics).

Arithmetic : Problems suggested by Geography and Science ; compare lengths of rivers, for examples in division ; value of wheat farms, quantity of wheat raised and its value at a certain number of bushels per acre ; the values of hides and income of trappers from that source ; value of cattle.

Language : The thoughts expressed on paper are taken from History, Science, etc.

Spelling : Words necessarily introduced by the other studies.

FIFTH GRADE

History : Story of John Smith (his struggles with the shiftless colonists, his adventures with the Indians, and his expedition of discovery).

Geography : Chesapeake Bay and vicinity ; oyster-beds, tobacco-raising ; coal and iron mines and fruit-growing in addition to study of climate, relief, soil, etc.

Science : Tobacco plant, oysters, clams, snails, with other native plants and animals of Virginia.

Arithmetic : Quantity of tobacco chewed by one person per year, in a lifetime ; quantity smoked ; its value.

Weight of ashes of cigar compared with weight of cigar ; one is what per cent of the other, etc.

Language : Compositions on the history of an oyster, the production of iron, John Smith's adventures, etc.

SIXTH GRADE

History : Causes of the French and Indian War.

Desire of France and England to secure the fur trade — differences in religion, etc.

Geography: Valley of St. Lawrence, the Great Lakes, Ohio River, Nova Scotia, and New Brunswick, Lake Champlain, and Lake George, pineries of West and North, fisheries on coast.

Science: Fur-bearing animals — beaver, otter, mink, bear, buffalo, raccoon. Also deer and moose.

Arithmetic: Relative size of the lakes, expressed decimally ; of the states in the once disputed territory ; relative worth of various kinds of furs, and so forth.

The third grand subdivision of Ziller's work, that of Methods of Teaching, is based on Herbart's four distinctions, CLEARNESS, ASSOCIATION, SYSTEM, and METHOD, as already explained in Chapter VI of Part I.

This topic is discussed in the next chapter.

CHAPTER V

METHOD IN TEACHING — THE FORMAL STAGES OF INSTRUCTION

ZILLER has given an exhaustive treatment of the principles laid down by Herbart under the terms CLEARNESS, ASSOCIATION, SYSTEM, and METHOD as explained in Part I, Chapter VI. He has, however, given a special function to the processes *Analysis* and *Synthesis*, in that analysis works upon present stores of knowledge and experience, in order to prepare the mind for the best possible apperception of the new material that is synthetically offered to it by instruction. Recognizing this separate function of analysis and synthesis, most followers of Ziller now divide the step *clearness*, as defined by Herbart, into *two* steps, thus making five in all. Dr. Rein names them as follows: (1) Preparation (analysis), (2) Presentation (synthesis), (3) Association, (4) System, (5) Application.

The following translation from Rein's *Das Erste Schuljahr* (The First School Year), made by Dr. Charles A. McMurry,[1] gives a perfectly clear idea of the subject as conceived by the disciples of Ziller: —

[1] *General Method*, Bloomington, Ill.: Public-School Publishing Co., 1893.

The Formal Steps in their Outlines — Proceeding now to the act of instruction itself, we notice first of all that the subject-matter of every study like arithmetic or geography is to be divided up into a number of smaller parts, units of instruction, each of which will occupy from one to four, or even more, recitations. These divisions of a term's work in history or geography are what Ziller calls *methodical unities,* and each one of them is to be carried through the successive steps of a systematic recitation plan, namely, the formal steps.

For if the single topics which go to make up the great variety of school studies are to be clearly understood and thoroughly assimilated, each must be worked over by itself. For this purpose sufficient time must be given so that the details of each object can be absorbed, and this absorption with the details must be succeeded by a period of recollection, a brief survey of the situation, a glance backwards and forwards, so as to fix the relations of this object to others. Suppose that the instruction in a class begins with one of these methodical unities. The first thing to do is to make plain to the pupils the great *object* or *aim* of the lesson. In a primary class, for instance, the aim may be so expressed: "To-day we will hear the story of a little girl that lost both father and mother." For a more advanced class as follows: "We are acquainted with the earth as a great ball hanging in space. We will next see whether this ball is at rest or in motion."

Reasons for stating the Aim at First — There are several important reasons in favor of the plain state-

ment of the purpose of a recitation at the beginning.
1. It pushes aside and out of view those irrelevant
thoughts which chance to occupy the mind before
the recitation, and it accordingly makes room for the
ideas about to be developed. 2. It transplants the
children into the new circle of ideas which are to
demand their attention, and it encourages the rise in
the child's mind of those older and kindred thoughts
which will be most welcome supports to the new ideas
about to be presented. 3. It excites expectation, and
this is the most favorable disposition of mind for the
beginning of instruction.   4. It gives the child a
strong incentive to an exercise of the will, and impels
it to voluntary coöperation in solving the difficulties
of the proposed lesson.

The last point is of fundamental importance, and
worthy of a special consideration. The pupil should
know beforehand what is coming if he is to bring all
his powers to bear on the work of learning, and it is
easier to call out all his effort if he knows beforehand
what is to be gained. To conduct a child along an
unknown road toward an unknown object, by means
of questions and hints, the object of which he does
not see, to lead him on imperceptibly to an unknown
goal, has the disadvantage that it develops neither a
spontaneous mental activity nor a clear insight into
the subject.

Having reached the end of such a line of thought,
the pupil looks about bewildered. He cannot survey the road that he has just gone over. He does
not comprehend what has happened to him. He stands
at the goal, but does not see the relation in which the

result stands to the labor performed. He does not rise to that satisfactory mental activity and favorable disposition of mind which are stimulated by the pursuit of a clearly set purpose. No aim, no will! Now since instruction that aims at moral character finds its highest purpose in the development of will power, it follows that a lesson should develop the will just as much as the understanding. But to develop will power, instruction must pursue plainly set aims, and to reach them the pupil must be called upon to throw all his mental powers into the *effort*.

The general purpose of a lesson having been made plain, the real work of teaching then begins, and in every methodical unity this work runs through a succession of five steps.

First Step — The first step in this process consists in a preparation of the ground for the reception of the new lesson. This is done by freshening up and calling clearly to the mind such older ideas as bear upon the new, such as by their similarity explain and assist the understanding of the new. It is only when a troop of old familiar ideas come forth to meet the strangers that they are received easily into the mind. It is in this way alone that they can make a lasting impression upon the thoughts and feelings. If these forces which lie asleep in the background of the child's thoughts are not called into activity, he will remain dull and indifferent to the recitation, and the instruction reminds us of a learned discourse which shoots over the heads of the listeners. Instead of interested attention and participation, it produces only weariness of mind.

This result will always follow when that which is said awakens no chords of sympathy in the minds of the hearers. If nothing springs forth from within to greet that coming from without, the lesson will be meaningless and the pupil unreceptive. Things new and strange can only be appropriated by means of a wealth of old ideas, and the plan of recitation must see to the preparation of these old materials during the first step.

Second Step — The second step begins with the presentation of the new lesson, which will vary in manner according to the age of the pupils and the nature of the study. A story will be related to a primary class, or developed according to the conversational method. A reading lesson for older pupils would be read. A geography topic would be presented by the teacher while talking and drawing, and a subject in physics while experimenting and speaking. If the preparation has been of the right kind the lesson will be appropriated with ease and certainty, and the teacher will not be compelled to talk and ask and explain all around the subject. Whenever this is necessary the preparation, *the first step*, must be regarded as a failure. What has been learned is not only to be momentarily understood, but permanently appropriated. It is necessary to close up this step with repetition and drill, and these must be continued under varying forms till the lesson has been firmly fixed. In this manner the first great act in the process of teaching and learning has been completed, namely, the presentation and reception of the subject-matter, and it consists, as we have seen, of two steps, preparation of the ground and presentation of the lesson. The second act within the limits of a methodical unity is the process of building up and bringing into distinct form the general or abstract ideas which are to be drawn from the concrete materials already collected, and this second act is brought to a conclusion in the three following steps.

Third Step — In the third step we are to bring together in the mind the newly won ideas, to compare them among themselves and with older ideas, and when necessary with additional new ones still to be presented; in short, to compare and to combine the new and the old. Such a comparison and union of ideas is necessary for two reasons: (1) in order that connection and harmony be established in one's range of ideas, and (2) that what is general and essential in the midst of special individual things may be extracted from them. Nowhere should heterogeneous heaps of knowledge, like piles of gravel, be brought together. Always and everywhere there should be an effort towards well-associated and systematized knowledge. "Our whole personality rests in the end upon the unity of consciousness, and this is disturbed and injured when the mind is driven through a confused conglomerate of knowledge in which unconnected ideas are piled up together."

But every concrete individual thing which is treated as a *methodical unity* contains or embodies a general truth, an abstract notion, which may be separated from the concrete thing in which it is embodied. But it can only be brought to light by bringing this object into comparison with other well-known concrete objects

which contain the same essential idea or truth, by
bringing together in the mind things similar but not
identical.   That which is common and essential to all
is strengthened by repetition, while accidental features
and differences drop easily into the background.   The
common truth which all the objects embody springs
forth as a new idea of higher potency, as a general
notion, as a rule or law.

Fourth Step — But the abstract idea is still bound
up with the concrete thing; a complete separation of
this abstract or general notion from its clothing in
particulars has not yet taken place: and this is the
purpose of the fourth step.   By means of a few well-
directed questions we call out into pure and simple
relief the general truth or rule, freed from its particular applications.   We reduce this idea to definite language expression, and finally bring it into systematic
connection with our previously acquired knowledge.
It only remains to impress the abstract ideas thus acquired upon the mind by repetition, so as to convert
them into a real mental possession.   With this the
process of abstraction is complete, but teaching cannot afford to end the matter here.   A fifth step is
needed to convert the knowledge acquired into use.

Fifth Step — Knowledge and ability to know have
of themselves no value either for the individual or
for society.   Knowledge must first step into the service of life.   One must know how to apply his knowledge.   Knowledge and power must be changed into
use; they must be transformed into conscious ability.
But will not this take care of itself ?   Not at all.
Hundreds of children have learned how to estimate

the surface of a triangle, and many of them can give the proof of the rule with ease and precision. But put the question to one of them, How many acres does a triangular garden with sides of a given length contain? he will stand helpless, unconscious of the fact that he possesses in his own mind the necessary elements for the solution of the problem. How is this explained? He has not learned to employ his knowledge. It is a dead possession. And are there not plenty of such cases? The conclusion is, that even the application, the use of knowledge, has to be learned. "Here also it is only practice that makes the master. But drill which aims only at mechanical habit is not sufficient. Even during school life that which is learned should be applied as often and in as many cases as the narrow limits of the child's life permit."

Since the value of knowledge culminates in use, instruction should cultivate its use so far as possible in a closing step called *application*. For this purpose the child should be held to a diligent use of its stock of ideas as rapidly as they are acquired, to go from the particular to the general, and back again from the general to the particular, to traverse his circle of ideas from a given standpoint in all directions, and to make use of the results reached for the solution of moral, theoretical, and practical questions. In this manner a child's acquired ideas may be so developed, so welded together in firm, systematic, comprehensive association, that all his knowledge becomes a reliable, personal possession. It is clear and systematic as well as practical.

To recapitulate: In the work of instruction each methodical unity should be carried through the following steps: —

1. It should introduce the new lesson by means of a preparatory discussion.

2. Present the new lesson.

3. Compare the new in its parts and with older ideas and their combination.

4. Draw out the general results of this comparison and arrange them in systematic form.

5. Convert the knowledge acquired into use.

This topic, more than perhaps any other from the Herbartian school, is now accessible in English. The reader is referred especially to the following-named works for an extended discussion: McMurry, *General Method;* De Garmo, *Essentials of Method;* Lange, *Apperception,* pp. 200–245; Rein (Van Liew's translation), *Outlines of Pedagogy;* Herbart (Felkins' translation), *Science of Education,* pp. 122–128. Concrete illustrations will be given in the next Chapter, where Dr. Rein's contributions are discussed. The varying terminology used by writers with respect to the formal steps of instruction is well presented in the following table, compiled by Van Liew in his translation of Rein's *Outlines of Pedagogy.*[1]

[1] Page 145.

FORMAL STEPS

I. Dörpfeld and Wiget.

1. Perception. (Percept.)
2. Thought. (Notion.)
3. Application. (Power.)

(a) Introduction.
(b) Perception. } Apperception.
(a) Comparison.
(b) Condensation. } Abstraction.

II. Herbart and Ziller.

1. Clearness. { (a) Analysis. (b) Synthesis.
2. Association.
3. System.
4. Method (Function).

III. Rein.

1. Preparation.
2. Presentation.
3. Association.
4. Condensation.
5. Application.

With the above may be compared the designations given to the "formal steps" by the following American writers.

I. De Garmo.[1]

1. Preparation — Analysis.
2. Presentation — Synthesis.
3. Comparing and uniting, or, Induction, Association (Socratic).
4. Formulation of Notional — Deduction; from which we descend again to particulars.

C. A. McMurry.[2]

I. Presentation. { 1. Preparation. 2. Presentation. 3. Association and Comparison.

II. Elaboration. { 4. Generalization or Abstraction. 5. Practical Application.

I. Apperception. (Sense-perception.) (Concrete illustration.)

II. Abstraction.

III. From Knowing to Doing — Application.

[1] *Essentials of Method.* [2] *General Method,* chap. viii.

Upon Ziller's work as a whole many judgments have been passed, both laudatory and the reverse. Certain it is, that few can regard it with indifference. Its bold, radical, far-reaching propositions challenge attention, even if they do not always command assent.

CHAPTER VI

DR. WILLIAM REIN—REDUCING THEORY TO PRACTICE IN ELEMENTARY SCHOOLS

So long as men merely lecture at the universities or write their opinions in their books, the world at large does not know whether their theories will work in actual practice or not.

When Dr. Stoy died at Jena in 1885, it was exceedingly fortunate for the cause of education in general, even if it was not for the specific doctrines of Professor Stoy himself, that Dr. William Rein, Director of the State Normal School at Eisenach, was called to be his successor. Dr. Rein has made the pedagogical seminary at Jena the most noted of its kind in Europe, to which students resort from every civilized country.

His specific contribution to the Herbartian cause lies not so much in the promulgation of new ideas, as in the practical application of the important ones that had remained mostly untried. Ziller's opponents were inclined to regard him as a pedagogical sentimentalist, who would sacrifice any number of rich educational inheritances for a poor mess of pedagogical pottage. Few teachers thought that his plan of concentration, with its scheme of culture epochs, and its subordination of the greater part of the subjects of study to Biblical and profane history, would stand the test of actual practice.   It was the unrivalled work of Dr. Rein, aided by two of his colleagues in the normal school, to show in eight single volumes corresponding to the eight years of the common schools, just how Ziller's plan for the selection and concentration of studies, could be carried out in practice, revealing at the same time in the most elaborate detail the methodical treatment of each subject according to the formal steps.   These eight volumes[1] are a monument of patient labor, such as only Germans are capable of executing.

As will be seen from the succeeding citation, Dr. Rein adheres closely to Ziller's exposition of Herbart. Concerning the principle of the culture epochs as a guide to the selection of studies, he announces the three following principles : —

1. By following the order of the national culture, and presenting it in the light of ethical judgment, we shall call forth permanent interest in the developing child; hence, *chronological progress from older and simpler, to newer and more complicated stages and conditions.*

2. As a basis for this material we must use childlike classical, religious, literary, and historical matter (Volks Stories and Robinson Crusoe in the first two grades).   "Periods which no master has described, whose spirit no poet has breathed, are of small value

[1] *Theorie und Praxis des Volkschulunterrichtes (Die acht Schuljahren)* by Rein, Pickel, und Scheller; Leipzig: Heinrich Bredt.

for education" (Herbart). Only classical presentations invite the pupil to constant and profitable repetitions; they alone furnish nourishment for the interests and aspirations of children. Only through these does the past speak in full tones to the present.

3. Only large, connected unities of subject-matter are able to arouse and keep alive the deep sympathy of the youthful mind, thereby contributing to the development of character. "Great moral energy is the effect of entire scenes and unbroken thought masses" (Herbart).

As a result of the application of the idea of Concentration to the work of the first year, Dr. Rein exhibits the following program: —

Studies: { 1. Core of Concentration } Drawing, Singing, Number, Reading, and { 2. Nature-Study } Writing.

1. *Ethical Core of Concentration* (*Gesinnungs-Stoff*); Grimm's Fairy Tales. These form the center, or core, of instruction. The other branches are concentrated about them; and by them the remaining topics are largely determined.

2. *Nature-Study* — All the subjects that are suggested by the Fairy Tales, receiving a special illumination from them and thereby awakening an intensified interest, are first chosen for treatment. School life and individual experience furnish much supplementary matter. (See list of object lessons below.)

3. *Drawing* — For this purpose the objects mentioned in the Fairy Tales and in the nature-study are used.

4. *Singing* — The choice of songs is determined by

the moods developed by instruction and by school life. The various songs must express emotion at fitting times.

5. *Number Work* — This is connected closely with the things that are considered in the various culture and nature subjects.

6. *Reading and Writing* — The material is chosen from the topics treated during instruction in Fairy Tales and Nature Study.

" For the following grades, also, we seek to apply the foregoing principles, even though the growing complication of the studies makes it more difficult than during the first year. *The more the studies threaten to diverge, the firmer must the fusion of the individual parts be made, so that through all multiplicity and variety, there shall never be lacking the fundamental condition for unity of consciousness, for identity of personality, and therefore for the development of moral character."* [1]

A noteworthy peculiarity proposed by Ziller and carried out by Rein and other members of the Ziller school, is that the ethical core of concentration for the first year shall consist of some dozen Fairy Tales from Grimm ; and for the second, of the story of Robinson Crusoe. This is done for the reason that they represent still more elementary culture stages than the simplest stories of the Bible, being, therefore, more perfectly adapted to the child's elementary stage of comprehension. This proposition was at first violently opposed by most teachers as a caricature on

---

[1] *Das Erste Schuljahr*, 5th edition, p. 87.

the religious teaching given in these grades of most schools where the Bible itself was used as the basis of all moral and religious instruction. The plan is now more calmly considered, though it has found but little practical application in the schools, the chief cause, however, of all the slowness of reform in German schools being that the curriculum is prescribed by state authority.

The stories are carefully edited before being presented to the children. A good idea of the general method of treatment may be seen from the following examples, translated from *Das Erste* and *Das Zweite Schuljahr:* —

THE WONDERFUL KETTLE

I

Once there was a very poor little girl, who lived with her mother near a great wood. They had nothing to eat, and grew very hungry. Then the little girl went out into the woods. Here an old woman, who knew already that the little girl was hungry, met her. So the old woman gave the little girl a kettle, and said to her, "If you say to the kettle, 'Kettle, cook,' it will cook you good, sweet rice. But if you say, 'Kettle, stop,' it will stop cooking." Then the little girl took the kettle home to her mother, and told her all about it. After this they did not need to go hungry, for as often as they pleased they ate good, sweet rice.

II

One day the mother went away from home, and left the little girl all alone. Soon she became hungry, and said to the kettle, "Kettle, cook"; but she had forgotten all about saying, "Kettle, stop." The kettle kept on cooking more rice, until it ran over. Then the kitchen became full of boiled rice, then the whole house, then the street, and at last all the houses. Nobody knew what to do.

At last the mother came home, and called out, "Kettle, stop." It stopped cooking at once; but whoever wanted to get into that town had to eat his way in through the rice.

Methodical Treatment

A. (1) I have told you about a little girl. Who had died? Could they give her food any longer? The poor girl must have often suffered hunger, why? What must she have had, not to be hungry any more? Children name many kinds of food. There are warm foods and cold ones. How are warm foods prepared? (Kitchen, stove, fire.) How long must rice cook? May it cook forever? What would happen?

I will tell you of a little girl who often had to go hungry.

(2) Story to "as often as they pleased, they ate good, sweet rice."

B. (1) What did the old woman give the girl? What was she to say to it? Could the mother say this, also? How did she know about it? What would the kettle do? How long would it cook? Do you suppose the girl had thought of this? If she had not, what would happen?

(2) Story to "and nobody knew what to do."

C. (1) How long will the kettle go on cooking? Who could stop it? Where is the mother?

(2) Story to the close. Repetition by children. Uniting of the three sections. Questions on the whole. Several pupils tell the whole story.

(3) The child had not remembered what the old woman had said. Who had? Has any one ever told you anything that you ought to notice and remember? (The teacher, parents, brothers, and sisters, etc. Children give examples.) Who had not forgotten what the old woman said? What could the mother do when the rice ran over? Who had forgotten it? Who did not know what to do? If you have forgotten something, what can you not do? But if you have remembered, what can you do? What does the teacher (papa, mamma) say when you have forgotten something? What should you not do? What should you do?

(4) "We must not forget what we are told to do."

(5) Application: *e.g.* What should you do when you meet the teacher? (Greet him.) When you meet people on the street? When your mother goes away and tells you something, what must you do? etc.

Robinson Crusoe is recast as is seen in the following translation of Rein's version, the original form not being regarded as important, since it must in any event suffer translation for German children. As soon as a section is narrated, it at once undergoes treatment according to the five steps described in Chapter V. All the studies of the second year are related to this ethical core as to the fairy tales of the first year. Following the story of how Robinson settled is a delightful account of an actual lesson on Robinson Crusoe told by Dr. Klemm in his *European Schools*.[1] It gives a vivid picture of the manner in which this material is utilized.

ROBINSON SETTLES

Among the things that Robinson brought from the ship were a spy-glass, a Bible, and pens, paper, and ink. He folded himself a book, in which he wrote everything that happened. At the same time he prepared an almanac. He set up a cross as a monument at the place where he had been cast upon the shore.

Robinson now began to build himself a secure dwelling. His tent stood on swampy ground, so he sought a better place and found one on high ground near a spring. Here there was a cave in the rock large and dry enough for him to live in. He first carried all his things to the cave. Then, wishing to protect himself, he made a strong fence by driving tall stakes close together in a half-circle. The fence reached from the rock near the cave around to the rock on the other side, and enclosed a space twenty paces long and half as wide. He left no opening, but climbed over the fence by means of a short ladder, which he always drew in after him. The fencing of his dwelling-place was a severe labor, and lasted from the 3d of January to the 14th of April.

Robinson now began to enlarge his cave into a kind of cellar. This took a long time, for he had neither

[1] New York: D. Appleton & Co., 1889.

pick nor shovel. But he found a piece of firm, hard wood from which he made a very good shovel. This took him three days.

Within his fortress Robinson now built a hut, for his tent let the water through when it rained. He drove stakes into the ground in front of the cave, put a cross-bar on top of them, and then used poles for rafters, which he placed standing against the rock above the cave. He covered the roof with branches of trees, leaves, and whatever he could find that would keep out the rain. The sides he covered with wood, plastering up the cracks with clay. The doorway he covered with a piece of sail cloth. But there was still plenty to do within. He had no bed, no chair, no table, and no fireplace. It took a long time to make these. Then he put his things in order. The most of them he put into the cave and the cellar.

To know the time of day, he made himself a sun-dial. After this he could divide his time regularly. Every morning he took a walk in the open air with his gun, then he worked until 11 o'clock, at which time he prepared and ate his dinner; from 12 to 2 o'clock he slept, since the heat of the sun was then unbearable. The remainder of the day he worked, writing in his diary at the end of the day.

One morning he shot a goat. At first he rejoiced, but how sorry was he, when he saw a kid by the side of its dead mother! He took the goat upon his shoulders and the kid followed, but would eat nothing, however much he might try to induce it to do so. At length he had to kill the kid to prevent it from slowly dying from starvation. At another time, he shot a young goat in the leg, caught it, carried it home, and bound up the wounded leg. The wound healed, and the animal became so tame that it never ran away. Afterwards the goat gave him rich milk.

At first when night came on, Robinson sat in darkness, or had only the light of the fire on the hearth. By and by he began to study how he could have a light, and found a way. He used the fat of the goats for oil, prepared a wick, and could now keep a small lamp burning, which he had brought with him from the ship.

A Lesson on Robinson Crusoe [1]

Teacher. " Well, my children, we heard that Robinson had at last found means to return home. He was ready to embark in the ship, the captain of which was willing to take him across the ocean. What do you think he took along with him ? "

Pupil. " I think he took his parrot."

Teacher. " Why ? "

Pupil. " Oh, he liked the bird, and he thought it would be a nice present for his mother."

Teacher. " Indeed, my child, he was sure to have taken his parrot, and I am glad he thought of that dear mother of his. Would you have thought of your mother first, if you had been in his place?"

Pupil. "Yes. Don't you know he had nearly broken his mother's heart by running away from home ? "

Teacher. " Well, what else did he take with him ? "

---

[1] Reported by Dr. L. R. Klemm in his *European Schools*, pp. 199–206.

Pupil. "I think he took Friday. He could not have left him alone on the island. He owed him thanks for being his companion."

Teacher. "True, we must never forget a debt of gratitude. He who forgets a friend is not worthy to have a friend. What else did he take?"

Pupil. "He took his self-made clothes and parasol, to show how he had helped himself."

Teacher. "Yes, it is likely that he took them. Anything else?"

Pupil. "I think he took the tools he had made, and some of the pots he had formed and baked."

Teacher. "The tools, yes, but hardly the pots, for he would have found it very troublesome to travel with them. So, then, they took leave of the island. The sun shone brightly, and the birds sang as though they meant to say good-by to Robinson and his black friend. They both went on board the large sailing-vessel, where they were well received. Now the anchor was wound up." (Teacher draws an] anchor, pupils explain its use.) "The sails were hoisted" (sails were drawn on the board, by pupils likewise on slate), "and the wind began to move the vessel onward. Robinson stood on deck and looked back to the island where he and Friday had spent so many weary months. Both remembered the many hardships they had suffered. Now some one may tell the story so far."

Pupil. "When the captain of the sailing-vessel had agreed to take Robinson with him to Hamburg,[1] Rob-

---

[1] Remember this was a German school. Another deviation from Defoe's original is found in the substitution of goats for llamas.

inson said to him: 'Let me take my friend Friday. He has been my companion for many months and years, and it would be ungrateful if I should leave him here alone on the island.' The captain was willing to take the black fellow also. Then Robinson took on board what was dear to him, his parrot, his tools, his clothes of goat-skin, and other things which he had wanted to show at home. He intended to give the parrot to his dear mother, the poor lady who had grieved for her bad, runaway boy. Both Robinson and Friday took leave of the places on the island where they had found shelter, and by taking the captain along on their tour of leave-taking they showed him the island and many of the objects that had served them. When they stood on the deck of the sailing-vessel they looked back upon the island. The sun shone upon the gently swaying palm-trees, the goats were capering among the rocks, and the birds sang and twittered as though they meant to take leave of Robinson," . . . etc., with delightful childish particularity.

Now another child told the story somewhat differently, a proof that each pupil thought his own thoughts. Then this part of the narrative was entitled "*Robinson's Departure from the Island*." This heading found a place on the blackboard under I.

Teacher. "For the present, children, we must leave Robinson on the ocean, and let us hope he will not meet with another storm such as had wrecked the ship on which he had left home. We have a gentleman with us who has been on the ocean several times. He comes all the way from America. Ask him how long it took him to cross the mighty ocean."

Pupil. " Oh, no, he cannot have come from there; he is not black or red like Negroes and Indians." Some boys laughingly agreed that the teacher's statement could not have been right. But others looked sober and one of them said: " My cousin went over to America some time ago, and when he comes back I hope he will be white yet. People don't get black there who are not born black." That sobered the others at once, and now they believed that there might be white people in America. After this fact was acknowledged the boys said to me, " Do tell us how long it took you to cross the ocean."

" It took me thirteen days and ten hours, but you see, I came in a large steamer. Had I been in a sailing-vessel, it would have taken me much longer — at any rate, several weeks."

Pupil. " Why, that's nearly two weeks! Did you not see any land on the way ? "

" Yes, on the tenth day we hailed the coast of England, and after that we hardly ever lost the coast out of sight, till we reached Hamburg."

Pupil. " Well, how long does it take a sailing-vessel to cross the ocean ? "

" If the wind is favorable, about five weeks. But it may take seven weeks."

Pupil. " Hooh! seven weeks; why that's forty-nine days, just think of it! Did you see any fishes ? "

" Yes, my dear, we saw large fishes, called tumblers, who jumped from one wave into another, following the steamer to eat what was thrown overboard. They are called hog-fish, because their flesh looks like fresh pork, rosy and fat."

Pupil. " Did you have any storms on the sea ? "

" Yes, a storm that lasted three days, and we had much fog, in which we could not see the bow of the steamer when standing at the stern."   Other questions with which I was pelted I will omit here and proceed with the lesson.

Teacher. " Let us see, boys ; our story tells us that Robinson had a passage which lasted nine weeks.   If you remember where Robinson's island is situated, west of South America, the voyage was very swift."   (Map is shown, and distances are compared.)   " The vessel met with no storm or fog, and the weather was fine. The fishes in the sea could be seen playing in the sunshine.   Robinson and Friday made themselves useful on board by helping to set sails and doing other things. At last they reached the coast of England, but did not land.   The vessel glided along the shores of England, France, Holland, and Germany, and finally up the river Elbe, and entered the harbor of Hamburg.   Some one may tell the story of *'Robinson's Voyage across the Ocean.'* "

First one, then two others, told the story, mentioning time of voyage, comparing it with that of a steamer.   The fishes, sunshine, wind, sails, work on deck, and other points were touched with a faithfulness truly astonishing.

Teacher. " Let us proceed.   Tell me what was done when the ship was fastened to the dock ? "

Pupil. " The people left the ship and went on land."

Teacher. " Leaving everything under deck they had brought with them ? "

Pupil. "No, they unloaded the freight."

Teacher. "What may that have consisted of?"

Pupil. "Well, the ship had been in the South Sea, and may have been loaded with oranges or other Southern fruit, perhaps with cocoanuts."

Teacher. "What other things are brought from foreign countries?"

Pupil. "Petroleum, wheat, dye-wood, wild animals, hides, dried fish."

Teacher. "Think of some things that do not grow in Germany."

Pupil. "Coffee, rice, tea, cane-sugar, cotton, tobacco."

Teacher. "Very well. Our story does not say with what the ship was loaded; but, when it was fastened to the dock, all the freight was carried out and wheeled into the big magazines along the dock, where the merchants came to buy. Shall we stay at the dock and see the freight unloaded, or follow Robinson and Friday into town?"

Pupil. "Let us follow Robinson."

Teacher. "All right; it must have taken several days to unload the ship, and Robinson wanted to hurry home to see his dear old mother. How do you think Friday behaved when they reached the harbor?"

Pupil. "Oh, he must have been very much astonished, for he had never seen a city. The many ships, the high houses, the many white people, and the smoking chimney-stacks of the steamers, the cranes for unloading ships, all of it must have looked very queer to him."

Another pupil. "The strangest things the savage saw must have been the horses drawing wagons. 'Look, Robinson,' he cried, 'look at these animals! did you ever see such strange things?' And when they entered a horse-car and noticed the long rows of houses with the many, many windows, the thousands of people on the streets, and all the many objects of interest flitting by, he sat in dumb amazement."

Teacher. "Very well told, my boy. I see I need not tell the story myself; you can tell it as well as I can. What happened when they left the street-car?"

Pupil. "Oh, Friday saw so many new things he had never seen before that he stood still every minute to ask Robinson to look at this and that." *Other pupils.* "Yes; and when they came to a big shop-window he wanted to know what everything seen there was for." "He reached out his hand to take some of the things, to look at them closer, but was much astonished to find he could not do that on account of the thick pane of glass between him and the articles." "I wonder how often he cried to Robinson, who was urging him on, to stay and look at a new article he had never seen?" "I believe he was afraid when he saw the first dog. He may have thought him to be a wild animal, such as a panther."

Teacher. "We will call this part of our story '*Their Arrival in Hamburg and Friday's Astonishment.*' Some one may tell me the story." It is repeated in a connected manner by several pupils. Then the teacher said: "Before we hear what Robinson found at home, let us repeat the three parts of our story. This section shall tell us of his departure from the island; the second section may tell us all about his voyage across the ocean; and the third of their arrival in the harbor and Friday's astonishment at the new sights he beheld." It was surprising to see how faithfully they recalled the different incidents spoken of and how well they expressed their thoughts.

Teacher. "At last they reached the house where Robinson was born. He looked at the door-plate, which used to bear the name 'Daniel Crusoe,' but now bore another name. Robinson rang the bell. A servant opened the door and asked him whom he wanted to see. He said, 'I want to see Mr. and Mrs. Crusoe.' 'They do not live here any longer, but wait a minute, I will call my master. He may tell you where to find them.' The gentleman came and looked at this strange couple, Robinson not having had time to shave his long beard and cut his hair, and Friday, the black fellow, must have looked odd enough in this city of white people; and then remember they were laden with queer-shaped things and a jabbering parrot. Robinson asked anxiously after his mother. The gentleman of the house asked them in, offered them seats, and told them all about the old couple.

"Robinson's mother had grieved so much over her runaway boy that she fell ill, and when news reached her that the ship in which he had sailed for foreign lands had been wrecked, she died of a broken heart. Think of the bitter tears of repentance Robinson cried when he heard that that dear, gentle, loving mother of his had died of grief! He was a strong man now, but the hot tears trickled down into his long beard, and for some time he could not control himself. Friday, seeing his friend's great distress, began to weep too; but the parrot that was intended for a present to the old dame did not know what to make of it. At last Robinson controlled himself enough to ask after his father.

"He was still alive, the gentleman said, but he had retired from business and lived in a small house near the harbor, where he sat, lonely and forsaken, to watch the ships coming into and leaving the harbor. Robinson thanked the gentleman kindly for the information, and left the old house to look up his father. After many inquiries along the wharf, he found the house where his father lived. They hurried upstairs, and in a tidy little room they found the old man. His hair had become white, his eyes dim, and his voice trembling. Robinson threw himself on his knees before him and told him he was that bad, runaway boy. He had been saved and had come back to him never to leave him again. The old man laid his hands on his son's head and thanked God for having given him back his boy.

"My readers may believe me if I say the pupils sat there spellbound, tears in their eyes, and many of them sobbing. The teacher had told the story so touchingly that the children's sympathy had been aroused. Not an incredulous smile, not a sneer was seen, not a word was heard from them for some moments after the teacher had closed his narrative. It was one of those moments in which it is said an angel walks through the room. At last the teacher roused the children from a deep reverie by asking them to repeat this part of the story, which he termed

' *Robinson's Bitter Repentance.*' It was done with
touching simplicity and great accuracy. Again the
entire lesson was reviewed, partly by questioning the
class, partly by allowing them to narrate portions in
a connected manner. Many new incidents were added,
and when at last the lesson closed, the story of Robinson Crusoe was finished to the satisfaction of all
concerned.

"This narration furnishes the 'Gesinnungs-Stoff'
(material for the sentiments) of this class as other
tales do in lower, and as Biblical history does in higher,
grades. Besides offering food for the sentiments,
these lessons increase the pupils' knowledge, give
opportunities for employing their hands, and polish
their language. Much of what is offered in a connected manner in the above account was given in
conversation, but a *verbatim* repetition might have
been tedious to the reader."

The following outline of nature- (and object-) study
as it is concentrated about the ethical core, shows that
the principle of presentation is by no means to be
sought in the subject-matter itself, but that it owes
its place to suggestions arising from the fairy tales,
about which everything is to be concentrated. The
sequence of topics is determined wholly upon psychological grounds, the apperception of the pupil as in-
fluenced by instruction in culture subjects being the
sole guide. Professor McMurry's plan of concentration found in Chapter IV, Part II, will fully illustrate
the manner in which these object lessons are related
to the central culture study.

OBJECT LESSONS FOR FIRST YEAR

Room. 4 walls (names), ceiling and floor. Protects from rain, wind, and cold.

Bed. We lie in bed when tired — sick. Soft and warm in bed. We will not be sluggards.

Clothing. Names of parts of clothing. We wear clothing, (1) that we may not freeze, (2) that we need not be ashamed, (3) for adornment, (4) for carrying things.

Food. (1) There is much that we can eat. (2) We eat many things raw, many boiled, roasted, baked. (3) There are foods from flour, flesh, milk, fruits, leaves, roots.

The Garden. (1) Shape of the garden (some particular garden). (2) Cannot live in the garden, for there are no walls and no roof. There are vegetables, grass, fruit, pleasure gardens. All gardens should be well kept.

The Field. (1) There are cultivated fields and meadows. (2) The field gives the field-animals living-place and food. (3) In the field grows also food for man. (4) But we cannot live in the fields, for we should not be protected from rain and cold.

The Wood. (1) Many trees stand close together. (2) In the woods it is pleasant and cool (in summer). (3) The trees keep off the rain. (4) The trees keep off the wind. (5) Berries and nuts grow in the woods. (6) One can easily hide in the woods.

The Heavens. (Sun, moon, stars.) Form, color, height, clouds. Sun by day. Moon and stars by night. Sun, round like a shield — shines — makes light, warmth — setting, rising. Dawn. Twilight. Moon, like sun — rises, sets — light — no warmth, changing forms — man in moon. Stars, like sparks — some larger than others — cannot count them — some men know them and their places (children know the evening star and the Pleiades, the North star, and the Dipper) — twinkle.

Directions. (1) Towards where the sun rises is East. (2) Towards where it sets is West. (3) Towards where the sun stands at midday is South. (4) Towards where the sun never goes is North. (The children turn and point to various directions.)

Schoolhouse. (1) Our schoolhouse has three stories. (2) In the first story are 4 rooms, in the second 3, in the third 2, etc. (3) School is held in the school-rooms. (4) We learn in the School.

The Well (Hydrant). (1) Well gives us water to drink, to wash, and to cook with. (2) The well gets water from the earth. (3) Fountains, wells with pumps, windlasses, etc., and hydrants.

Flock of Sheep. (1) The sheep is a mammal, for the little lambs suck milk from the mother sheep. (2) The sheep a good and patient animal, for it does not kick or bite, and does not become angry even when beaten. (3) The sheep is a useful animal, for it gives us its wool and its flesh.

Coal. (1) Coal is a fuel. (2) With coal we heat the room — cooking-stoves. (3) We have charcoal, soft coal, and hard coal.

The Bean. (1) Shape of the blossom of the bean. (2) The beans oval shape and sharp-pointed. (3) Beans grow in pods. (4) The pods open into two parts. (5) Beans serve us as food.

Waters of the Neighborhood. (1) The river is a great flowing water. (2) The brook is a small flowing water. (3) The pond is a still-standing water. (4) The river has two banks, the pond a bank all around. (5) Bridges are built over rivers. (6) In the water are fishes. (7) The river drives mills and floats ships and boats.

Chickens. (1) Chickens are useful animals. (2) They give us their eggs and their flesh. (3) The cock crows when the day begins to break.   (4) The hen is a good mother to the little chickens.

The Squirrel. (1) The squirrel is a lively little animal. (2) It can jump and climb well. (3) It is a gnawing animal. (4) It lives mostly in trees. (5) It likes pine seeds and nuts best.

The Duck. (1) The duck is a swimming bird. (2) It is useful. (3) It gives us its eggs, feathers, and flesh.

The Mouse. (1) The mouse is a little mammal. (2) Is a gnawing animal.

The Goat. (1) The goat is a useful animal. (2) Has two horns and a split hoof (cloven hoof). (3) Is a ruminant (chewer of the cud).

The Wolf. (1) Is a wild, ravenous beast. (2) Is a beast of prey. (3) Sometimes attacks man.

The Fox. (1) The fox is a sly, cunning animal. (2) He catches poultry and kills other small animals.

The Farmyard. (1) Yard, (2) house, (3) barns, (4) granaries. In the house the farmer and his family live, the animals in the stalls, in the loft is the hay, in the granary the grain.

Snow and Ice. Winter — cold — ice glittering, first thin then thick, sliding, skating. Don't go on ice too soon. Ice flowers on the windows.

Christmas. (1) Christmas tree, presents, etc. (2) Christ wishes all little children to be good. (3) He desires to have them come to him when they die.

The Bear. (1) The bear is a beast of prey. (2) He is a carnivorous animal. (3) He is a cave-dweller. (4) What tricks he can perform.

The Wren. (1) The wren is the smallest singing-bird. (2) Likes best to stay in hedges and thickets. (3) Eats flies, spiders, caterpillars, and berries. (4) Sings his little song in summer and in winter. (5) Is a cunning bird.

The Hunter. (1) What animals does he shoot? (2) How does he load his gun? (3) Guns dangerous for children to handle. (4) What good do his dogs do?

The Church. (1) The Church is a large house. (2) Many benches, altar, steps, organ. (3) In the Church people sing, the preacher prays and preaches. (4) On Sundays people should go to Church.

The Donkey. (1) The donkey is a useful animal. (2) Has a single hoof. (3) Used for drawing and carrying. (4) Is slow but sure. (5) Brays.

Dog and Cat. (1) Useful home animals. (2) Are mammals. (3) The dog is a watcher, our servant, companion, play-fellow, trickster; The cat is our mouse-trap. (4) The dog is true, the cat treacherous.

The Horse. (1) Horse our largest home animal. (2) Has a whole hoof. (3) Is a beautiful, clean, and wise animal. (4) His food is grass, clover, hay, oats, and corn. (5) Used for drawing and carrying.

Though the *Acht Schuljahren*, containing elaborate expositions of the Herbart-Ziller theories of selection, concentration, and methods of presenting the various studies of the curriculum, and at the same time setting forth the entire content of what is to be taught, are to be regarded as the masterpiece of Professor Rein's activity, yet he has published many works of a less comprehensive nature.[1]

In connection with a report of the Practice School at Jena, Dr. Rein gives us a detailed program of concentration for the sixth grade of an elementary school, a sample of which is given as follows : —

[1] One of the latest, his *Grundriss der Pädagogik*, has been recently translated by Dr. C. C. Van Liew, of the Illinois State Normal School at Normal, Ill., under the title *Outlines of Pedagogy*. It may be obtained of C. W. Bardeen, Syracuse, N.Y.

COÖRDINATED CURRICULUM.—A. HUMANISTIC STUDIES

TIME.	I. HISTORICAL INSTRUCTION.		II. ART INSTRUCTION.		III. LANGUAGE.		
	1. BIBLE HISTORY. (2 hours per week.)	2. PROFANE HISTORY. (2 hours per week.)	1. DRAWING. (2 hours per week.)	2. SINGING. (2 hours per week.)	1. GERMAN. (3 hours.)	2. LATIN. (6 hours.)	3. FRENCH. (3 hours.)
15-19 April	Israel under the kings. Saul: The people demand a king.	Greek history. Historical material taken from the age of mythology.	Hellenic architecture. Treasure house of Mycenae.	Songs of Spring.	(a) Content, Form, Essay: Our visit to the Preller gallery.	(a) Form, Irregular verbs. (b) Content, Stories of Grecian myths.	Analytical preparatory course. Repetition and drill for fixing the series.
21-26 April	Saul anointed king. Victory over the Ammonites.	The same continued. Gods and their worship.	The same continued. Lyon gate at Mycenae. Cyclopean buildings. Doric order. Visit to architectural museum.	Songs of Spring.	(a) Content, "Hope," by Geibel. (b) Form, Copy essay. Corrections, Dictations.	(a) Form, Translation from German into Latin. (b) Content, Roman myths.	The same continued. Formation of series for pronunciation.
April 28 to May 3	The same.	Persian war. Battle of Marathon.	Triglyph of the Parthenon.	Songs of Spring.	"Hope." (b) Form, Correction of Dictation.	(a) Form, Review, Translation into Latin. (b) Content, as above.	New group: About hotels.
5-10 May	Jonathan and the battle with the Philistines.	The same continued.	Triglyph continued. Doric capital.	Songs of Spring.	(a) Content, Poem, Pleasures of Travel. (b) Form, Dictation, Apposition, Punctuation.	(a) Form, Continuation. (b) Content, Continuation.	About theatres.
12-17 May	Samuel lays down his office. Saul's disobedience.	Results of battle. Militiades's end.	Doric capital.	Songs of Spring.	(a) Content. Pleasures of Travel (cont.). (b) Form, The day after the Battle of Marathon.	(a) Content. Miltiades in Nepos. (b) Form. Review of grammar.	Continuation: Collection of groups.
19-24 May	Saul is rejected.	Destruction of Eretria. Review.	Base of the Doric column.	Songs of Spring.	(a) Content. Thunder storms. (b) Form, Dictation.	(a) Content, Life of Miltiades, Continuation. (b) Form, Continuation.	(a) Content, from the Life of Hercules. (b) Form, Recording the groups.
2-7 June	Saul and David. David becomes king.	Ionian revolt. (a) Darius against the Scythians. Land and people of Scythia.	Front tile of the Parthenon. Discussion.	Songs of Spring.	(a) Content. Corrections. New Essay. Trip to Schwarzburg in the letter form.	(a) Content, Miltiades (Battle of Marathon). (b) Form, Review of grammar.	(a) Content. Hercules. (b) Form. Notebook on system. Rules of pronunciation.
9-14 June	The same continued. Goliath and David.	(b) The same continued. Histiæus and Miltiades.	The same continued.	Songs of Spring.	(a) The stars. (b) Essay, Corrections.	(a) Miltiades. Nepos plenior 10, 11. Battle of Marathon. (b) Grammar. Review.	(a) Hercules. (b) Notebook: était and avait.

COÖRDINATED CURRICULUM — (*Continued*). — *B.* NATURE STUDIES

TIME.	1. GEOGRAPHY. (2 hours.)	2. NATURAL HISTORY. 1 P.M. outdoors. (1 hour.)	3. ARITHMETIC. (2 hours.)	4. GEOMETRY. (1 hour.)	5. PRACTICAL WORK. (1½ hours.)	GYMNASTICS.
15-19 April	Greece: Peloponnesus: Position, boundaries, form.	Garden and field: First stage, cultivated plants. Garden work.	Decimal system.	Triangles. Theorem of the outer angle.	Work in school garden: raising of plants to be studied.	Drill and outdoor exercises. Free gymnastics.
21-26 April	Peloponnesus: Relief, climate.	Seeds: Sprouting observed in garden.	Oral work in addition of decimal fractions.	Continuation. Sum of the outer angles.	Doric order. Triglyph.	Staff drill. Horizontal bar. Jumping.
April 28 to May 3	Peloponnesus: continuation. Landscape descriptions.	Continuation, and establishment of a herbarium.	Continuation.	Continuation.	Continuation.	Gymnastic drill for order. Parallel bars. Jumping.
5-10 May	Continuation.	The garden in bloom. Observation of blossoms.	Continuation.	Continuation. Inner and outer angles of quadrilateral.	Doric capital (see Drawing).	Marching. Staff drill. Climbing and horizontal bar
12-17 May	Middle Greece. Megara, Attica.	Review and summary of matter learned. The germs of plants.	Subtraction. Oral addition continued.	Continuation.	Continuation.	Staff. Parallel bars. Swing rings.
19-24 May	Continuation. Beotia.	Continuation. Recording the results in notebooks. Further observation in growth.	Oral subtraction. Written work in addition.	Conclusion.	Completed.	Staff. Horizontal bar. Jumping.
2-7 June	Continuation. Phocis.	Stalk of grain. Leaf with axil. Tendrils of peas. Development of the potato.	Continuation.	(a) Work: exercises in measurement: (b) System: cases of coincidence.	Plan for front tile from the Parthenon.	Free gymnastics. Horizontal bar. Horse.
9-14 June	Continuation. Locris. Doris.	Gathering up and recording results.	(a) Work: comparison of heights in geography. (b) Subtraction of decimal fractions.	(a) As above. (b) Law of Coincidence.	Same projected.	Continuation. Rope jumping.

CHAPTER VII

DR. KARL LANGE — APPERCEPTION [1]

It is the incomparable service of Dr. Karl Lange, Director of the Higher-Burgher School, at Plauen, Germany, to have shown in a genial, concrete manner the close dependence of education as an end upon psychology as a guide. To him belongs the credit of elucidating a psychological method by which every problem of the school-room can be directly examined. Hitherto most of our attempts to make psychology applicable to teaching have been at the best formal and mechanical, because we have presented psychology as a sum of more or less isolated theories or doctrines of special phases of mind. Going into the school-room with a schematized body of psychological distinctions (true enough it may be, but unimportant as a guide to education), our teachers for a time try to be psychological; but they soon abandon complicated systems

---

[1] *Apperception*, a Monograph on Psychology and Pedagogy. By Dr. Karl Lange, translated by Elmer E. Brown, Charles De Garmo, Mrs. Eudora Hailmann, Florence Hall, George F. James, L. R. Klemm, Ossian H. Lang, Herman T. Lukens, Charles A. McMurry, Frank McMurry, Theo. B. Noss, Levi Seeley, Margaret K. Smith, and edited by Charles De Garmo. D. C. Heath & Co., Boston, 1893.

for simple common sense. But Lange opens up new
possibilities by sending the teacher into the class-room
with all his psychological knowledge concentrated —
focussed upon one point, — the mental processes of the
living child. *All learning is apperceiving.* How shall
I select the subject-matter of the studies? Study the
ends of education and the manner in which the child
best apperceives. How shall I articulate the instruction? Study the same problem for the relations of
knowledge. How shall I present the lesson and conduct the recitation? See what order will best conduce
to understanding and interest. What means shall I
take to impart high ideals, or to secure right disposition, or reliable habits of conduct? Go to the same
fountain of pedagogical guidance — the apperceiving
mind of the child.

More successfully than any of his fellow-workers,
perhaps, Lange has succeeded in showing how this
pedagogical insight may be acquired. How important
it is that modern teachers should have this truly scientific guidance in their work is set forth in the following extract from the introduction to the translation
of Lange's *Apperception :* —

"It is now evident that if we are to make further
progress in education we must add to this initial impulse given by Pestalozzi something of the scientific
spirit of the age in which we live. A number of facts
point to this conclusion. In the first place, the curriculum of studies is no longer the simple thing it was
in Pestalozzi's time. Study after study has been
added in obedience to some popular demand or because
of the esoteric interest of the schoolmaster. What

now constitutes our curriculum is a chaos of isolated subjects, which are allowed, not from any demonstrated psychological need, but because of some popular or professional demand. The only proper way to determine which shall be eliminated, which abridged, is to submit the whole to a thorough investigation according to the well-developed psychology of the present time, since the primitive systems are wholly inadequate to the task. Such an investigation will necessarily take into consideration the educational value of each subject, when it has received the best possible coördination with other branches; it will consider the natural interests of the child, his power of comprehension, the effect of his present acquirements, disposition and leading purposes upon his acquisition of new knowledge, for all of these things will help to decide how the curriculum shall be made up. This is a problem not to be solved by efforts aroused merely by emotion or instinct, for the problem is essentially scientific in its nature.

" We meet this same need for the scientific application of psychology to education in another direction. As long as only the well-to-do classes were educated, there were many influences to which we could appeal to obtain the desired results. Were the child inclined to evade our instruction in order to follow his own devices, we might appeal to his ambition, to emulation, to pride, to shame, to regard for the reputation of family, and the like; but when the streets, the mines, the factories, the tenement districts, send their children to school, these indirect means of securing attention to study are mostly futile. We stand face to face with naked ignorance and indifference, and must make our impression in a few short years or suffer defeat. We can no longer rely on indirect means for arousing the mind to educational effort, but must contrive to awaken a deep, permanent, and growing interest in the acquisition and possession of knowledge itself. This is a psychological problem involving the child's acquirements, his natural instincts and interests, the content of the studies, together with an investigation into the time, order, and manner of presenting them. It appears self-evident, therefore, that to the primal inspiration for the uplifting of humanity, we must now add the intelligent direction of psychological science." [1]

The Monograph consists of three parts: 1. The Doctrine of Apperception; (*a*) Nature and Kinds of Apperception; (*b*) Conditions of Apperception; (*c*) Significance of Apperception in the Mental Development of Man.

2. The Theory of Apperception in its Application to Pedagogy. (*a*) The Object that is apperceived (Choice and Arrangement of the Subject-matter of Education) ; (*b*) The Subject that apperceives (Investigation, Extension, and Utilization of the Child's Experience) ; (*c*) The Adequate Union of these Two Factors in Instruction (Methods of Instruction).

3. History of the Term Apperception. (*a*) Leibnitz, (*b*) Kant, (*c*) Herbart, (*d*) Lazarus, (*e*) Steinthal (*f*) Non-Herbartian Psychologists, (*g*) Wundt.

The following citations from the discussion of the nature and kinds of apperception show to some

[1] Lange's *Apperception*, p. 6.

extent the spirit and method of the investigation: —

"Man enters life as a stranger; he knows nothing of the world that receives him: it is to him a new, unknown country, which he must explore, which he must conquer. How is this to be done? Nature assails his senses with a thousand allurements; she sends the rays of light that she may open his eyes to the innumerable things of the outer world, she knocks upon the door of the human spirit with excitations of tone and touch and temperature and all the other stimulations of the sensitive nerves, desiring admission. The soul answers these stimuli with sensations, with ideas; it masters the outer world by perceiving it." [1]

"This activity of the perceiving mind, however, explains another important fact. It is a well-known experience that one and the same object seldom occasions precisely similar perceptions in the minds of different people. Of the same landscape the poet's image would differ greatly from that of the botanist, the painter's from that of the geologist or farmer, the stranger's from that of him who calls it home. In the same way, one and the same speech is often understood in as many different ways as there are hearers. What does not the child see in his toys, the devout mind in the objects of its devotions! What does not the experienced reader of human nature see in the wrinkles and folds, the wilted and weatherbeaten features of a human face! How much do the gestures, the play of features, the glowing or fading

[1] P. 1.

fire of the eye, tell him of the battles and storms of
the soul! And the artist, does he not perceive in a
work of art a thousand things that escape the closest
attention of the ordinary observer? Has not each of
us the sharpest kind of an eye for the objects with
which our calling makes us best acquainted? In the
voices of nature the youthful lover of birds, like
man in the state of nature, hears the emotional and
volitional utterances of related beings, while the
Malay says of his bamboo forests, from whose
branches the wind entices the most manifold tones:
'The forest organ plays for each his favorite tune.'[1]

" In order that a sensation may arise, there is, as a
rule, a fusion or union of its content with similar
ideas and feelings. With the assistance of the latter,
the sensation is held in consciousness, elevated into
greater clearness, properly related to the remaining
fields of thought, and so truly assimilated.

" We call this second act in distinction from that
of simple perception or the reception of a sensation,
APPERCEPTION, or mental assimilation. This is a
psychical process which has a validity beyond mere
subjective perception, and is of the greatest significance for all knowledge, yes, even for our whole
spiritual life.[2] Let us see, therefore, the laws according to which this process is completed.

[1] P. 3.
[2] The inquiring mind is likely to ask at this point: Is it possible
to have *perception* without *apperception*? We may say in general
that knowledge is necessary for the assimilation of knowledge, and
this is the side of apperception of most importance to us as teachers,
but some are curious to know how, according to this, knowledge
gets a start. The author has shown at the beginning that a spon-

"Suppose we have the rare phenomenon of an eclipse of the sun. Rays of light of varying strength come from the lighted part of the sun's disk, and fall upon the retina of the eye. A physical process arising outside of the body affects at once our nerves of sight. Hereby the peripheral ends of these nerves are stimulated to an activity that is conducted as a nerve excitation to the central ends of the nerves and there causes a specific change (excitation of the ganglion cells), which is characterized as the release of the nerve-excitement. This is a physiological process, which in time and cause seems bound up with the physical one, but which is in its nature entirely distinguished from it. To these external processes, and conditioned and occasioned by them, is now added a pure inner activity, which seems to have nothing in common either with vibrations of ether or with nerve

taneous activity on the part of the soul in accordance with its own nature must be presupposed in order that we may have any experience at all. In the case of the bell, for instance, the vibrations of the air are contributed by the object, but the mental response that we know as *sound* comes from the mind itself. In this way it is possible for a knowledge of sounds to start, without there having been any previous experience of sounds to serve as interpreting ideas. We have thus in distinction from the apperception in which knowledge is involved a *primary* apperception, without which we should never know anything. As a rule, Herbartian writers emphasize the cognitive phases of apperception, in which new knowledge is assimilated by the products of our former experience, in the form of knowledge, feelings, purposes, interests, etc., partly because these are the phases of the subject of practical importance to pedagogy, and partly from the implications of the Herbartian system of psychology. A careful study of the historical sketch at the close of Lange's book will reveal to the reader the attitude of the various thinkers in respect to this topic.

currents; it is the reaction of the soul, a sight-sensation. This is the psychical act with which the perception closes. We naturally receive from the continually changing disk a variety of sensations, which, united and related to the same object, give us a picture of the eclipse of the sun; this is a subjective perception.

"Only a new-born infant, in so far as it may be supposed to see at all, could stop at this stage in the perception of the outer impression. During the first months of life a human being would perceive this rare celestial phenomenon with dulness and indifference, and without understanding or interest. He will at this stage have nothing to add to the given impression; he will indeed not be aware of all that is to be seen, so that he can take away none particularly.

"It is very different with the adult. He gains from the same phenomenon of nature a far richer, sharper, and clearer perception. We notice not only the gradual eclipse of the sun, but we recognize also its cause. We see a dark disk enter the sun's field of light, and say to ourselves that this is the unilluminated side of the moon, which in its passage around the earth, is now passing between us and the sun, and whose cone of shadow hides from us the star of day. To this we add the comforting certainty, that all this has to do with right things, that the eclipse is proceeding according to known and fixed laws — a thought that goes far to remove a large part of the emotion-stirring power of this unusual occurrence.

"Whence comes this perception, so rich in content and clear in outline? It has evidently arisen under the influence of the related thought content, with which we have met the outer impressions, and under the influence of the observations and knowledge that we have formerly gained through instruction, reading, and personal observation of the heavenly bodies and their movements. It was with the help of what we already knew of this keenly expected natural event, and of similar reproduced ideas, that we created this new perception and placed it in an orderly position in the organism of our knowledge, so that it now forms a clear and definite part of the same. WE APPERCEIVED IT. Not unessential is the service rendered by the will, which is here led by intellectual feelings. As we were viewing the astronomical event with close attention, it not only correctly adjusted the sense organs for the observation, but it removed disturbing ideas as far as possible from consciousness and admitted only such as were favorable for the assimilation of the new. This was accompanied by a corresponding physical effort, viz., that of tension, which made itself felt in the sensation. At the moment of successful apperception, as would appear from Wundt's investigations, the sensory nerve current was transferred from the central ends of the nerves to a region lying in the front part of the large brain, which is reckoned to be the apperception center. From here the excitation was partly directed back to the sensory centers, whereby there was a strengthening of the perception, and partly conducted further to the muscles of the eye, in which certain feelings of tension arose.

"Reviewing now the parts of the process to be observed in the act of perception, we find an extraordinary number of them: sense and motor stimuli, sensations of sight and muscles, reproduced ideas, activities of feeling and will — all these are exercised in the production of an apparently simple result without our being conscious of the action simultaneously. There are, however, two chief activities to be distinguished in the whole process. We perceive in the eclipse, first, just what the original constitution of our minds necessitates, even if they were no more developed than the mind of an infant. In this way a PERCEPTION arises. But through the ideas and skill obtained by former experience, we observe much that remains hidden to the inexperienced, and we add to the subjective perception numerous psychical elements from our well-stored minds, which were not immediately given in the observation. The mind apprehends outer impressions in accordance with the wealth of knowledge gained through former activity. THE PROCESS OF PERCEPTION BECOMES ONE OF APPERCEPTION." [1]

Even the moral nature is largely dependent upon the apperception of ideas, as the accompanying citation shows : —

"While the child is growing intellectually, he is making progress ethically as well. We have already seen that the ruling sphere of ideas and emotions determines in the main the moral insight of the human being. He usually judges his own moral worth and that of others according to what he himself loves, or what he wishes and longs for for himself.

[1] Pp. 5–8.

There is, therefore, no doubt that in early youth, as well as in infancy, the *feelings and interests of sense* influence to a considerable extent the moral consciousness of man. Indeed they can become the one controlling group of ideas among bad and uneducated children; with these anything is permissible that pleases. On the other hand, in the case of the well-trained child, they are subordinated more and more to the ideal example of the parents. He no longer follows blindly this authority, to which he has always been subject. But by comparing them with other persons and with his own imperfect being, he comes gradually to feel an unlimited reverence for his parents, which makes voluntary obedience toward them a duty, and causes their example to be regarded as a model. And soon other authority is associated with theirs; namely, that of teachers, near relatives, leaders among school companions, and masters with their servants. Especially in sacred history does God, the Perfect and Just One, appear as the highest authority, whose supreme will and control impress themselves indelibly upon the pupil's mind. *These are the examples which especially determine his moral conceptions, and hence control his apperception on moral questions.* They are vividly in mind when he acts; *they are his conscience.* Not as though he were unable to distinguish for himself what is good or bad. He knows unworthy deeds or worthy motives in themselves very well, entirely apart from all thought of what his parents, or teacher, or God would say on the matter. But such pure, independent moral feelings and judgments do not appear at this stage of

development in the abstract, but rather in connection
with certain model examples. Just as the thought
of a child in all spheres of knowledge deals in part
with very imperfect general pictures, not with general
concepts, *so in the field of ethics his morality does not
show itself effective in the abstract form of the idea, —
the principle, — but in the concrete form of the ideal.*
When one observes closely what guides the moral
judgment in early youth, one finds that, in most
cases, the example of some real person closely related to the child consciously or unconsciously exerts
a deciding influence in the apperception, and thus
largely determines the will." [1]

In his discussion of the selection and arrangement
of the studies Lange gives a thoroughgoing critique of
Ziller's position, differing from him in important particulars, yet acknowledging much truth in his presentation. The following citation summarizes Lange's
position: —

"Let us now sum up briefly the requirements that
have revealed themselves in reference to the object of
apperception. In general this direction holds good:
Offer to the child always that knowledge for whose
thorough assimilation the most favorable conditions
are present or easy to create.

"How can this be done?

"1. Such materials of knowledge must be chosen as
lie close to child experience in general, and likewise
to the consciousness of the people, *i.e.*, the subject-
matter of national culture.

"2. They must, as regards content and form, take

[1] Pp. 79, 80.

into consideration certain peculiarities of the child's intellectual development.

"3. They are to be arranged in such a manner that every topic shall create for the following ones numerous strong aids to apperception; *i.e.*, according to historical sequence (Law of Propædeutics).

"4. The various parallel subjects of the curriculum are to be arranged in such a manner that in each grade as many as possible allied topics may be associated, so that what is related in fact, may be related in the consciousness of the child (Law of Coördination, or Concentration of Studies).

"In so far as the simultaneous realization of the foregoing requirements does not meet insurmountable difficulties they may be regarded as valid. And indeed in most cases they will support and confirm one another. Yet the possibility is by no means excluded that one or the other of these requirements will clash with the rest. Certain material may be chosen in accordance with the historical principle, which in content and form expects too much from the child at a certain epoch of his development. Or the unequal rate of historical progress in the different branches does not admit of a useful concentration in the instruction. And the case is also conceivable that, in the realization of the third and fourth requirements, the intrinsic value of the subject-matter for instruction might not receive its full due. In all these cases it is advisable to limit one requirement by another, as far as is necessary, and not to lose sight of the chief principle while considering special applications. This refers to the last two directions; while the first two, which have reference to given, unchangeable facts, cannot be subjected to any limitation. It does not lie within the province of this discussion to sketch a complete curriculum of studies in accordance with the foregoing principles, even for one grade of school. Only a few practical conclusions may be permitted to us in connection with these general requirements." [1]

With the Herbartian conception of certain necessary stages in all rational methods of teaching Lange is in substantial accord, though his fine perception of the eternal fitness of things warns seriously against allowing teaching processes to be conducted mechanically according to formulas, however excellent in themselves. His book closes with a brief history of the term *Apperception* as it has been used in the history of philosophy.

Were there no other useful book among the myriad Herbartian publications, this one gem would justify the existence of the whole number, so genial, so true, so helpful, so inspiring is it in its treatment of the main problems of education.

[1] Pp. 132, 133.

CHAPTER VIII

DR. KARL VOLKMAR STOY — LEADER OF THE CONSERVATIVE HERBARTIANS

PROFESSOR STOY was born in Pegau, Saxony, in the year 1815. He attended school in Meissen, and studied at the universities of Leipzig and Göttingen. At the latter place he attended the lectures of Herbart, who inspired him with a love of philosophy and pedagogy. After closing his work as a student, he began teaching in Weinheim in 1839, going to Jena in 1842, where in the following year he qualified as *privat docent* in Philosophy. About the same time he took charge of a local private school, which under his leadership attained a high reputation. Pupils gathered to it from all over Europe, the survivors among them rejoicing even yet in the thoughts of their school days under their beloved principal.[1] In the year 1845, Dr. Stoy was made a Professor at the university. In 1865 he moved to Heidelberg; during the year 1867 he established a normal school at Bielitz in accordance with Herbartian principles, returning to Jena in 1874, where he remained until his death in 1885.

[1] Compare Wiessner, *Herbart's Pädagogik*, p. 105.

The greatest monument of his work in Jena is the pedagogical seminary, with its accompanying practice school, now so ably presided over by Dr. Rein. One of the peculiarities of this seminary is that it is an organic part of the university, receiving a yearly stipend from the state.

The Professor of Pedagogy is the real head of both seminary and practice school, though there is a headmaster in the practice school who presides in the absence of the Professor. There are three distinct meetings held each week at which the presence of all the students belonging to the seminary is required. The first is called a *Pratikum*, which consists of one or two model recitations conducted by student-teachers of the practice school. This exercise is not to be an examination of the pupils, but a typical illustration of the art of instruction. Each member of the seminary makes full notes upon the exercise, one of the number being appointed to bring in later a written critique of the whole performance. The *Pratikum* is held on Wednesdays.

The second meeting, called *Theoretikum*, is held in a classroom of the university, being conducted by the Professor. At this conference the time, usually one hour, is devoted to the discussion and elucidation of such technical or special questions as have arisen in the practice school during the week. Many of these concern the principles of methods, the treatment of special difficulties in discipline, the mental condition of individual pupils; further, the examination of special books on methods, of school text-books, and the laying out of programs of study. Often a student is appointed beforehand to bring in a written paper upon an assigned topic.

The writer well remembers the first task Professor Stoy set him, when as a student with small knowledge of German, he entered the university of Jena. It read as follows: "Psychological Analysis of the Observation of Natural Objects." After long labor over English psychologies, and the greater labor of putting the results into German, even with the assistance of Herr Theo. Storch, a charitable fellow-mortal, the paper was at length read before the wondering students. The Professor was very kind in his total rejection of the whole as a mechanical and valueless piece of work. He finally dismissed the paper by saying that it was merely an *observation about* a psychological analysis of the observation of natural objects, not an *analysis* at all.

The *Theoretikum* was held from seven to eight P.M. on Fridays. Immediately upon adjournment, the seminary reassembled in a room of a neighboring hotel, where an apartment was always held in readiness for it on this evening of the week. This meeting was called the *Conference*.

In Dr. Stoy's time, some twenty persons were usually assembled at that hour, seated about long tables arranged in the form of the capital letter T. Behind the cross-table at the head of the room sat Dr. Stoy upon the inevitable German sofa. The purpose of the *Conference* was to hear the reports of the critics upon the recitations that had been conducted on the previous Wednesday at the *Pratikum*. After a few preliminaries the person who presented the model

recitation read a written self-criticism of the effort, telling what he had tried to do, his methods of procedure,
and his own judgment as to the degree of success he
had obtained. This was followed immediately by the
report of the appointed critic, who usually went into
details, fortifying his conclusions by facts and argu-
ments. As soon as the reading of this critique had
been concluded, the person whose work was under examination replied to his critic, either acknowledging
the justice of his criticisms, or showing reasons why
he did not regard them as valid. At this point, the
discussion was thrown open to students and teachers
alike, each speaking upon whatever point seemed to
him most worthy of comment. The *Conference* lasted
until 11 o'clock, when it was closed by Professor Stoy
himself with a masterly review of the whole discussion.

The *Encyclopedia of Pedagogics* is Stoy's chief
work. The first edition was issued in 1861, and the
second, enlarged and amended, in 1878.   Besides
these may be mentioned *School and Life*,[1] *House Pedagogy in Monologues and Addresses*,[2] *House and School
Police (Government)*,[3] *Two Days in an English Gymnasium* (1860), *Organization of the Normal School*,[4]
Home Geography and Instruction in Language,[5] and
many articles in the *Schulzeitung*, whose editor he
was from 1870 to 1882.

Stoy's service to the cause of didactics is more a

[1] *Schule und Leben*, 1844.

[2] *Hauspädagogik*, 1855.

[3] *Haus-und Schulpolizei*, 1856.

[4] *Organization des Lehrerseminars*, 1869.

[5] *Heimatskunde und Spruchunterricht*.

vigorous restatement of Herbart's doctrines than a
contribution of new ideas.   The subject of instruction he treats under three heads, — Statics, Propædeutics, and Concentration.

1. Of the Statics of instruction, he says that there
must always be provision made for intellectual, ethical, and religious training, and that food for these
three chief interests must always be provided in the
program.   We must care for soundness of heart quite
as much as for soundness of head.   A certain proportion must consequently always be observed among
the three kinds of material — a static consideration.

2. Propædeutics.   Since only by the utilization of
present stores of knowledge and experience can any
instruction hope to succeed, it follows that he who
instructs without heeding this law of apperception
" plays on a harp without strings."   Every step taken
must, therefore, be a preparation for the next one,
forming its indispensable basis.   Everything that
could lessen the activity and association of ideas
must consequently be vigorously avoided.   The special principles of this forward (dynamic) view of instruction must be sought in the psychological study
of apperception and apperceiving interest.

3. Concentration.   If the statics of instruction determines the juxtaposition of studies, and the propædeutics the succession, both together constituting
" the two dimensions of instruction," there yet lies
in the enormous extent of possible and even needful
subject-matter a necessity of a peculiar kind, at first
of a negative character.   There arises the necessity
of repelling everything that could disturb the re-

awakening, the facility and connectedness of ideas, so that the problem arises of promoting to the greatest possible degree, unity of basal knowledge, connection of that which is related, and the association of supplementary ideas, so that time and strength may be economized. To explain how this can be done is the business of concentration.

But with concentration in Ziller's sense, Professor Stoy, with the partisanship known only to rival German professors, would have nothing to do. He regarded the whole plan as an exaggerated and visionary scheme. To his friend Dr. Bartel in Gera he wrote: "I should be thankful to you if, in the interest of truth, you would take occasion to say that I have nothing to do with Ziller's novelties. I regard them as harmful exaggerations, as wrecks from the great structures of Herbart. I am in harmony with you when, in conclusion, I express my final judgment: Everything new in this Ziller business is not good, and everything good in it is not new."

As a summary of Stoy's position, together with that of his sympathizers, the following points may be recapitulated: —

1. He holds fairly to the Herbartian basis of metaphysics, psychology, and ethics.

2. He accepts in the main the idea of historical development as a guide to the presentation of the culture subjects.

3. He rejects unconditionally Fairy Tales and Robinson Crusoe, which with the disciples of Ziller form the core of concentration for the first and second years.

4. He rejects with even greater emphasis Ziller's scheme of concentration, whereby all the other subjects of the curriculum are to be grouped about an ethical core of concentration, consisting for the most part of Biblical and profane history, with an introduction of Volks lore and Robinson Crusoe.

5. He believes in the formal steps of instruction as a rational guide to teaching.

Stoy himself was small of stature, homely of feature, eccentric in behavior and dress; but kind of heart, earnest of purpose, and helpful always to those who sought him,— a man whose memory is held dear by many hearts.

CHAPTER IX

DR. OTTO FRICK, LATE DIRECTOR OF THE FRANK-ISCHEN STIFTUNGEN IN HALLE

APPLICATION OF HERBARTIAN IDEAS TO SECONDARY EDUCATION

IF to Dr. Rein and his co-workers belongs the credit of applying Herbartian principles to the work of the elementary schools, it is to Dr. Otto Frick and his fellow-laborers that we must ascribe the credit of applying them to secondary education. What Rein does on the Ziller basis for the Volks schools, Frick has done on the Stoy basis for the gymnasiums. Nor is it strange that Dr. Frick should with Stoy reject the Ziller plan of concentration, for in the advanced classes of the gymnasium, to conduct natural science as subordinated to literature, history, and religion, would be to caricature the whole subject of science, making it conform to principles not its own. Men made a dismal failure of science when they taught it by literary methods; if in addition to this they had selected and arranged it according to the laws of literary selection and sequence, it would have presented a sorry spectacle. Natural science, at least in its higher stages, is not amphibious, living as well in one element as the other.

Dr. Otto Frick was the son of a preacher in Brandenburg, and was born at Schmitsdorf in the year 1832. After completing his university education at Berlin and Halle, he became Director of the Gymnasium at Burg. In 1880 he was appointed Director of the *Frankischen Stiftungen* at Halle, a most responsible position and one offering a wide range for pedagogical observation and experiment. This school, founded for the poor, especially orphans, two hundred years ago by Francke, now comprises a series of schools having some four thousand pupils and students of all grades and conditions of life. Almost every variety of school known to the German system is here represented, — Gymnasium, Real Gymnasium, Normal School, Volks Schools, Burgher-schools, Higher Girls' Schools, Orphan Schools, and the like.

It was the writer's good fortune to be associated with Dr. Frick for two years in a local branch of the *Verein für Wissentschaftliche Pädagogik*, which met two evenings in each month for the discussion of pedagogical topics from the Herbartian standpoint. He was a large, fine-looking man, of grave demeanor. Whenever he spoke, one listened as to a master. Although independent in thought, he was yet generous to opponents, and not slow in recognizing their strong points. From Herbart he differed mainly on psychological grounds. He could not join him in regarding the soul as the empty meeting-place of ideas, but was disposed to ascribe a considerable content to the soul itself, aside from ideas gained through experience.

There is, he thought, a distinct constitution of mind itself, which should be recognized in education. It was a serious loss to the teaching profession when this able, industrious man was cut off in the prime of his usefulness by sudden death, in January of the year 1892.

In educational theory Dr. Frick agrees so nearly with Professor Stoy that a separate exposition of their views is hardly needed. His opinions may, however, be found in his two monographs, *Didactic Principles,*[1] and *Unity of the School.*[2] Dr. Frick's service to the cause of education is not to be measured, however, by these monographs, but rather by the quarterly magazine, *Lehrproben und Lehrgänge aus der Praxis der Gymnasien und Realschulen,*[3] which he and Gustav Richter established in 1884, and which he edited until his death in 1892. This magazine, as its name indicates, is devoted to the selection and arrangement of studies, and to extended expositions of the methods to be pursued in every variety of subject. It constitutes a rich mine of didactic treasures, all bearing more or less clearly the Herbartian stamp.

Dr. Frick's contributions, especially upon historical and theoretical topics, greatly enrich the magazine. After eight years of constant discussion, he presented in the twenty-eighth number what he calls the outline of an organically arranged course of study for a classical gymnasium, in which each subject or group of

---

[1] *In wieweit sind die Herbart-Ziller-Stoy 'schen Didactischen Grundsätze für den Unterricht an den hohern Schulen zu verwerten.*
[2] *Einheit der Schule.*
[3] *Verlag der Buchhandlung des Waisenhauses,* Halle, Germany.

subjects has a rational development, and in which there is as much coördination as the age of the pupils and the nature of the subjects demand. In his view the gymnasium is an institution whose domain lies in the three great fields of education denominated with us as elementary, secondary, and higher. Dr. Frick divides the gymnasium course of nine years as follows : —

1. ELEMENTARY. First two years, age of pupils from 10 to 12 years.

2. SECONDARY. Next four years, age of pupils 12 to 16 years.

3. HIGHER. Last three years, age of pupils 16 to 19 years.

The Elementary stage is looked upon as a preparation for the more serious work involved in the Secondary one, while the Higher stage is regarded as the proper one for the systematic, rational coördination of related studies. It is hardly worth while to try to make infant philosophers, the task being not only impracticable, but also undesirable. Children readily form a network of associations among various studies if the connections are brought to consciousness; but we must wait until the stages of higher education are reached before there can be any intelligent grasp of far-reaching interrelations. This being the case, the course of study laid out by Dr. Frick, though by his wish to be regarded as tentative and illustrative, may be regarded as one of the most carefully planned programs ever printed. It purports to be rather an organization than an aggregation of studies. In it he has had three things constantly in mind, viz.: —

1. The Selection of Material.
2. The Sifting of Material.
3. The Articulation or Coördination of Material.

The courses as arranged by Dr. Frick will now be represented. It will be noted that form studies, like mathematics and grammar, are not inserted, not because they do not have to be taught, but that they may not obscure the view of the other subjects. Following the course will be found some expository remarks.

COURSE OF STUDY FOR A GYMNASIUM

.A. Elementary Studies — Two Years — Age 10 to 12

SEXTA — FIRST YEAR

Geography. — (1st Semester.) The typical geographical concepts illustrated by the home environment. Introduction to understanding of Relief, and the reading of a map. General lessons upon the globe.

(2d Semester.) Division of the earth into land and water. General descriptive view of all the continents.

Natural History. — First introduction into systematic observation of plant and animal life, according to chief types as found in the child's environment. (Biological home studies.) In summer the plants, in winter the animals, are brought to the front.

Enlivening of the geography heretofore presented.

Opening up of the home environment. The awakening and cultivation of the feeling for nature and home surroundings.

History. — Preparatory introduction into the chief typical forms of historical life. (The simplest social communities.)

(1st Semester.) The Odyssey (Grecian heroic age). First opening up of the antique world and its geographical theatre.

(2d Semester.)   Niebelungen Tales (German heroic age).   First opening up of the German ancient world and its geographical theatre.

German. — (The center of instruction.)   A National Reading Book, Part I (with an appendix of the local or home environment), for extending and deepening the impression and concepts obtained in local geography and natural history.   Pictures illustrating local traditions.

Latin. — Meurer, Pauli Sextani liber (that is, connected reading material concerning home regions ; extension into the Roman world or connected lessons from Roman History, perhaps a history of the kings, standing midway between tradition and history, or between patriarchal and heroic times).

Religion. — Biblical History of the Old Testament.   (Time of the Patriarchs, Heroes, Judges, Kings.)   Personal relation of the same (the community) and of the whole Israelitic people to God.   The most general facts of the Catechism are learned from the Bible History, especially the first Article and the Ten Commandments.

QUINTA — SECOND YEAR

Geography. — Lands.   More minute description (with an emphasis of geographical types).

(1st Semester.)   Home province, and state, and the whole of Germany.

(2d Semester.)   The remainder of Europe.

Natural History. — Extension of observation to neighboring regions in order to enlarge the observation of plant and animal life according to important types.   Extension of study to foreign lands.

In summer and winter as in Sexta.

History. — A closed circle of typical pictures from ancient, middle, and especially modern national history.   (Preparatory excursion through German history for a general conception of the whole ; essentially the history of kings and emperors, with pictures of cities, state, and national organization.)

German. — A National Reading Book, Part II, corresponding to
Part I for Sexta, but with stronger emphasis upon national
history, legends, and historical poems from ancient and
mediæval German history. Characterizations of great historical personalities therein considered.

Religion. — Bible history of the New Testament, the middle
point to be the life of Jesus as well as his personal relation
to God. General conception of the kingdom of Heaven as
the highest social community. The Catechism as in Sexta,
especially the second Article, the Lord's Prayer, and the
formulas used in baptism and at the communion service.

B. SECONDARY STUDIES — FOUR YEARS — AGE 12 TO 16

QUARTA — THIRD YEAR

Geography. — Land divisions. Extended description (with emphasis of types) of non-European countries. Especial
study of German colonies.

Natural Science. — Elementary and General. (1st Semester.)
Physical geography.

(2d Semester.) Geology (according to the scope and
treatment of the subject in the books of Geikie-Schmidt).

History. — Grecian history in thoroughgoing manner. A careful selection and a rounded period of the elements of
historical life. (Types of historical observation and conception.)

German. — The Franco-Prussian War of 1870–71, in a form
prepared for schools. A few of the most important war
poems ; then furnished with material from Grecian history
and culture, *e.g.* Geibel, Schiller (Ring des Polykr., Kraniche
des Ibycus).

Latin. — Cornelius Nepos. Chosen lives of warriors and states-
men, particularly of Grecian history (or a suitable preparation of the same material).

Religion. — Characteristic types of heroes, evangelists, apostles,
in accordance with evangelical and apostolic history, in the

center Paul (his personal relation to Christ and God). The beginnings of the Church and a general idea of the same. Catechism, third Article. Systematic treatment and elaboration of the first three.

TERTIA B — FOURTH YEAR

Geography. — From General Geography. (1st Semester.) The atmosphere, air currents, temperature and rainfall. Climate. The sea currents — most important lines of commerce (from Commercial Geography).

(2d Semester.) Plant and animal distribution according to characteristic types and differences.

N.B. Always (1 and 2) with repetition and utilization of previously obtained knowledge of the various countries.

Natural Science. — Systematic connected view of the most important organisms and laws. (1st Semester.) Plants.

(2d Semester.) Animals.

History. — Roman history as in Quarta. As a new type for observation and study we have the forming of the empire (Imperium Romanum).

German. — Reading Book with complete selections. The German Napoleonic Wars (with especial utilization of local traditions), and the songs of this period.

Latin. — Cæsar, Bello Gallico (the personality of Cæsar, the oldest conditions of the Gallic and German races in their connection with the Roman world). Struggle for independence, with a background of geographical and ethnographical facts. (Preparation for Tacitus, Germanica and Annals.)

Ovid, Metamorphoses. Choice of complete selections with a view to historical and culture epoch.

Greek. — Xenophon, Anabasis. Background of military and world's historical view — interest in individual personalities ; geographical and ethnographical pictures of civilization (as in Cæsar), involving regions through which the pupil is led in Bible and apostolic history, the Trojan legend, Herodotus, Curtius, and the Crusades.

French. — A reading material as in the French Reading Book upon the history of the German Napoleonic Wars, by Chr. Ufer, Altenburg, 1887. Illumination of the epoch through French sources.

Religion. — (1st Semester.) The history of the Apostles read. (Elaboration of the matter presented in Quarta.)

(2d Semester.) View of the wider extension of the Christian Church (Augustinus, Bonifacius, Luther). The Catechism completed and review of the organization of the whole (compare L. Schlutze, *Katechetische Bausteine,* 1887).

TERTIA A — FIFTH YEAR

Geography. — From General Geography. (1st Semester.) Mineralogy, where possible, with utilization of home observations, together with an introduction into the most elementary ideas in chemistry.

(2d Semester.) Consideration of the earth as a seat of life ; its relations to the other heavenly bodies.

Natural Science. — Introduction to Physics. Employment of knowledge acquired in Quarta.

History. — (Through Secunda B and A.) German history in elaborate presentation. Elaboration of the separate epochs presented. The historical observations and conceptions obtained in *Quarta* and *Tertia B* are enlarged and deepened through careful elaboration in the development of the German people. The opposition between Church and state is new, as is also the growing world-commerce ; the entire instruction has intimate regard for the geographical background.

German. — Archenholt's Seven Years' War. Frederick the Great (a group of selected situations and types), exhibited through materials chosen from the history of this war. Schiller's Ballads (in arrangements and groupings as connected wholes).

Latin. — Curtius, Rufus. Alexander the Great (individual personalities of world-wide renown ; geographical and ethnological background). Ovid, Metam. Selections (pictures of inner life ; psychological motive, cosmogony and age of the world).

Greek. — As in Tertia B, the preceding class (in all events a glance through the whole up to the arrival in Trebizond).

French. — Michaud I and (or) III, Croisades (selections). Further elaboration of the preceding. Mœurs et Coutumes des Croisades.

Religion. — Synthesizing outline. (1st Semester.) General view of the divisions and subdivisions of the Scriptures, the Church songs (species and origin), the important religious ideas, doctrines, and dogmas.

(2d Semester.) The idea and essence of God's kingdom. Its embodiment in the Church (organization of the Church year of divine service ; extension and activities of missions), always with temperate treatment based upon written testimony.

SECUNDA B — SIXTH YEAR

Geography. — Not a subject to be taught, but a principle to be observed at every opportunity.

Natural Science. — Physics with the closest possible association with the geographical conception to be further impressed or newly learned.

History. — See preceding class.

German. — (1st Semester.) Goethe, Hermann und Dorothea. Schiller's Wilhelm Tell.

(2d Semester.) Schiller, Jungfrau von Orleans, and Maria Stuart.

Latin. — Livy, History of the Kings and the beginning of the Free State (the development of a state).

Cicero, de imperio Cn. Pompeii (the first preparations for the monarchy), pro Ligario (Cæsar dictator).

Virgil, Æneid. Selection (Fall of Troy).

Greek. — Xenophon, Hellenica, chosen selections. The beginning of Athenian power. The Odyssey. Selections for an outline of the whole.

French. — (1st Semester.) Jeanne d'Arc, by Borante (as a
preparation for Schiller's drama and for introduction into
a significant era of French. English history. Wars for
freedom).

(2d Semester.) Maria Stuart, by Lebran (for the same
reason).

Religion. — (1st Semester.) Lessons from selected historical
portions of the Old Testament (the personality of Abraham,
Moses, Joshua, the Judges, and the Kings).

(2d Semester.) The Gospel of Luke in the original, with
synoptical side views of the other Gospels.

N.B. Compare with Secunda A, the next class.

C. HIGHER EDUCATION — AGE FROM 16 TO 19

SECUNDA A — SEVENTH CLASS

Geography. — Not a subject to be taught, but a principle to be
observed at every opportunity.

Natural Science. — (1st Semester.) Elements of Chemistry.

(2d Semester.) Physics.

History. — See Tertia A.

German. — (1st Semester.) Niebelungen Lied (und Gudrun).

(2d Semester.) Heliand, Walter von der Vogelweide
(selections — natural feeling, knightly service, Kaiser songs,
God's service).

Latin. — Livy. Selections for an outline of the Second Punic
War. Cicero, pro Archia, de Amicitia ; Virgil, Æneid.
(Selection, Shield of Æneas. Outlook into the Rule of
Augustus. Eclogue IV.)

Greek. — Herodotus. Selections to give an outline of the whole
Persian War. Odyssey. Selections for an outline of the
whole.

French. — Suitable selections for an introduction into the
history of the French Revolution (Mignet) and of Napoleon (Thiers, Bonaparte en Egypte, etc., and from Lan-
frey).

Religion. — (1st Semester.) Lessons chosen from poetic and philosophic portions of the Old Testament.

(2d Semester.) Lessons from the easier Epistles of Paul.

N.B. As in Secunda B, careful presentation and association of fundamental Biblical and Christian ideas.

PRIMA B — EIGHTH YEAR

Geography. — None taught.   See preceding class.

Natural Science. — (1st Semester.) Outlines of Mathematical Geography.

(2d Semester.)   Physics.

History. — (For this and last class.)   Mediæval and modern history.   Synthesis of the important conceptions of historical life.   Use of the preceding treatment, together with various lessons from original sources, supplementing of the latter.   Constant review of geographical knowledge.

German. — (1st Semester.) View of the inner development of German literature.   Parzival.   Klopstock's Messias, and Odes (selections).

(2d Semester.)   Lessing.

Latin. — (1st Semester.) Tacitus Germania, and Selections from the Annals, Lib. I and II (the German struggle for liberty).   Germanicus and Arminius.   Horace, Odes (selections).

(2d Semester.) Cicero, de Oratore (selections: nature and purpose of oratory) ; Horace, Odes (selections).

Greek. — (1st Semester.) Thucydides.   Pictures from the Sicilian Expedition, Funeral Oration of Pericles, and as contrast and reverse, glimpses of the downfall of the Hellenic world, III, 82, 83.   Writings of Thucydides concerning his conception of the end and purpose of history. The Iliad.

(2d Semester.)   Demosthenes, the Iliad, Sophocles' Antigone.

French. — (1st Semester.) Montesquieu, Considérations.

(2d Semester.) Racine, Athalie.

Religion. — (1st Semester.) Lessons on the Gospel of John
(the personality of Christ).

(2d Semester.) Lessons upon the Epistle to the Romans
(personality of Paul).

PRIMA A — NINTH AND LAST YEAR

Geography. — Not taught. See remark in Secunda B.

Natural Science. — (1st Semester.) Physics.

(2d Semester.) Conception and nature of the Cosmos
("Nature as a whole moved and quickened by an inner
power").

History. — See preceding class.

German. — (1st Semester.) Goethe.

(2d Semester.) Schiller. Impressive gathering up of the
important fundamental ideas presented in the instruction
in German.

Latin. — (1st Semester.) Cicero, pro Sestio (Fall of the Roman
Empire). Tacitus, Annals, Selections from Liber I (Rise
of the Cæsar rule. Augustus, Tiberius, and the royal
house). Horace, the Roman and Kaiser Odes.

(2d Semester.) Cicero, de Natura deorum, Somnium Scipi-
onis, Horace, Ars Poetica.

Greek. — (1st Semester.) Plato, Apology and Crito (the pedagogical mission of Socrates to the people), the Iliad.

(2d Semester.) Phædo, the Iliad, Sophocles' Ajax.

French. — (1st Semester.) One classical comedy (Molière).

(2d Semester.) Oratorical prose and an article on the
history of literature. Outlines of the development of French
literature.

Religion. — (1st Semester.) Selections from Luther's writings.
His Catechism.

(2d Semester.) Careful review and synthesis of matter
already learned, particularly Biblical and Christian fundamental conceptions.

Remarks on the Course of Study

1. The historical interest is the backbone of the whole body of higher education; the interest in national history being of first, and that in ancient history of secondary, importance. This being the case, it is natural that the environment of the pupil, local, state, and national, should receive the chief emphasis; and that next to this the Greek and Roman culture should be emphasized. It is to the instruction in history and to that of native and foreign literature that we are to look for the cultivation of this interest.

The reading matter in the mother tongue is depended upon to preserve the unity of the course through the studies touching the home environment of the child. Literary selections first emphasize the last great German war (1870-1), and then go back to the Napoleonic, the Seven Years', and the Thirty Years' wars, the Reformation, etc., the object of the whole being that a clear understanding of German manners and customs, German homes, history, legends, and poetry, shall be placed in the center of the whole realm of instruction. This, it will be remembered, is the substance of the demand of the German Emperor, when he said the schools should produce young Germans, not young Greeks and Romans; yet Dr. Frick advocated this plan long before the Emperor spoke.

2. A thorough sifting of the material of instruction can be obtained only by confining it to that which pertains to great periods and epochs, to really great personalities, to the typical and characteristic, the

truly classical. Such a limitation results in dropping whole subjects at certain stages; thus, for example, Geography is omitted after Tertia A, Latin Grammar after Secunda B, and Greek Grammar after Secunda A.

3. In addition to the coördinating influence of history and literature, the following aids to the same end may also be named: —

(1) Unity of treatment is preserved within each important subject or groups of subjects. Thus, for instance, the whole of natural science is to be taught with its manifold relations clearly in view, a technical isolation of the various topics, like botany, zoölogy, geology, etc., being avoided.

(2) The natural intimacy existing between such subjects as geography and natural science, and between these and literature, and that between physics and mathematics, is continually brought to the consciousness of the pupil.

(3) The favoring of such subjects as involve at once a wide range of events and a broad stretch of country, the Odyssey, the Niebelungen Lied, the Seven Years' and the Thirty Years' wars, for illustration. Almost every part of Germany has a local interest in some phase of the Thirty Years' war.

(4) The search for and the selection of organic bodies of knowledge pertaining to individuals, to communities and states, are to be constant; so, too, is the emphasis of middle or turning points in the events pertaining to individuals or communities, to whole historical epochs; or even to the development of important ideas.

(5) The constant regard for the mind and feeling

of the pupil, which is the true center of instruction, is to be ever held in mind. His apperceptive capacity must be observed, his permanent inherent interests developed.

Scores of prominent German schoolmen and professors have done Germany service in the work of adapting the Herbartian pedagogics to the needs and conditions of the German schools. It would not, however, add to the value of this exposition to confuse the typical work of the leaders already presented with a host of variations. It must suffice to mention in the appendix the chief works of others who have become noted on account of contributions to the cause, whether in psychology, ethics, or general and special theory of education.

PART III

HERBARTIAN IDEAS IN AMERICA

CHAPTER I

THE HERBART CLUB

THIS Club was organized at the Saratoga meeting of the National Educational Association in 1892, and consists, for the most part, of teachers who have made a special study of Herbartian principles of education. The purpose of the Club is to facilitate the spread of these ideas, and to promote their rational application in school work under American and English conditions. The Club has made a beginning by the translation of Lange's *Apperception*,[1] already mentioned in Part II, Chapter VII, and by the translation of Ufer's *Introduction to the Pedagogy of Herbart*.[2] These works are translated by members of the Club, and edited by the writer of this volume.

Previous to the formation of the Club, however, the present writer issued two books based on Herbart. The first, *Essentials of Method*, an analytical treatment of the formal stages of instruction, was issued in 1889; while the second, a translation of Lindner's *Empirical Psychology*, appeared in 1890.[3]

[1] *Apperception*, a monologue on Psychology and Pedagogy, by Dr. Karl Lange. Boston: D. C. Heath & Co., 1893.

[2] Boston: D. C. Heath & Co., 1894.

[3] De Garmo's *Essentials of Method*; Lindner's *Empirical Psychology*. Boston: D. C. Heath & Co., 1893.

Other important translations are as follows: —

1. Herbart's *Psychology*, by Margaret K. Smith, Oswego, New York State Normal School, 1891.[1]

2. Rein's *Outlines of Pedagogics*, by C. C. and Ida J. Van Liew, Illinois State Normal University, 1893.[2]

3. Herbart's *General Pedagogics and Moral Revelation of the World*, by Henry M. and Emmie Felkin, of England, 1893.[3]

A beginning has been made in the work of adapting Herbartian principles to American conditions. A course of illustrative lessons arranged according to the Ziller plan of Concentration, prepared by Dr. Frank McMurry while professor of pedagogy in the University of Illinois, has already been presented in Chapter VI of Part II.

The most extensive contribution of this kind has been made by Dr. Charles A. McMurry, of the Illinois State Normal University, at Normal, Ill. In 1892, he published *The Elements of General Method.*[4] This work is a sympathetic exposition of the principles of Herbart as interpreted by Ziller and Rein, with copious use of fitting illustrations drawn from Anglo-Saxon history and experience. In his discussion of the relative value of studies he has the following to say of the fetish of formal culture, or discipline of the mind by a few studies like grammar and arithmetic: —

[1] International Education Series. New York: D. Appleton & Co., 1892.

[2] C. W. Bardeen & Co., Syracuse, N.Y.; also Swan Sonnenschein & Co., London.

[3] D. C. Heath & Co., Boston; also Swan Sonnenschein & Co., London.

[4] Bloomington, Ill.: Public School Publishing Co.

"The second article of faith is a still stronger one. The better class of energetic teachers would never have been won over to formal studies on purely utilitarian grounds. A second conviction weighs heavily on their minds. '*The discipline of the mental faculties,*' is a talisman of unusual potency with them. They prize arithmetic and grammar more for this than for any direct practical value. The idea of mental discipline, of training the faculties, is so ingrained into all our educational thinking that it crops out in a hundred ways and holds our courses of study in the beaten track of formal training with a steadiness that is astonishing. These friends believe that we are taking the backbone out of education by making it interesting. The culmination of this educational doctrine is reached when it is said that the most valuable thing learned in school or out of it is to do and to do vigorously that which is most disagreeable. The training of the will to meet difficulties unflinchingly is their aim, and we cannot gainsay it. These stalwart apostles of educational hardship and difficulty are in constant fear lest we shall make studies interesting and attractive and thus undermine the energy of the will. But the question at once arises: Does not the will always act from motives of some sort? And is there any motive or incentive so stimulating to the will as a steady and constantly increasing interest in studies. It is able to surmount great difficulties.

"We wish to assure our stalwart friends that we still adhere to the good old doctrine that 'there is no royal road to learning.' There is no way of putting aside the great difficulties that are found in every study, no

way of grading up the valleys and tunnelling through
the hills so as to get the even monotony of a railroad
track through the rough or mountainous parts of education. Every child must meet and master the difficulties of learning for himself. There are no palace
cars with reclining chairs to carry him to the summit
of real difficulties. The *character-developing power*
that lies in the mastery of hard tasks constitutes one
of their chief merits. Accepting this as a fundamental
truth in education, the problem for our solution is,
how to stimulate children to encounter difficulties.
Many children have little inclination to sacrifice their
ease to the cause of learning, and our dull methods of
teaching confirm them in their indifference to educational incentives. Any child, who, like Hugh Miller
or Abraham Lincoln, already possesses an insatiable
thirst for knowledge, will allow no difficulties or hardships to stand in the way of progress. This original
appetite and thirst for knowledge which the select
few have often manifested in childhood is more valuable than anything the schools can give. With the
majority of children we can certainly do nothing better than to nurture such a taste for knowledge into
vigorous life. It will not do to assume that the aver-
age of children have any such original energy or
momentum to lead them to scale the heights of even
ordinary knowledge." [1]

The chapter is summarized as follows : —

"*History* in the liberal sense surveys the field of
human life in its typical forms and furnishes the best
illustrative moral materials. *Nature study* opens the

[1] *General Method*, pp. 45, 46.

door to the real world in all its beauty, variety, and law. The *formal studies* constitute an indispensable part of useful and disciplinary knowledge, but they should occupy a secondary place in courses of study because they deal with the *form* rather than with the *content* of the sciences. It is a fundamental error to place formal studies in the center of the school course and to subordinate everything to their mastery. History and natural science, on the contrary, having the richest knowledge content, constitute a natural center for all educative efforts. They make possible a strong development of will-energy because their interesting materials furnish strong and legitimate incentives to mental activity and an enlarged field and opportunity to voluntary effort in pursuit of clear and attractive aims." [1]

One of the most suggestive portions of the *General Method* is the part of the chapter on "Culture Epochs" that discusses the function of history in an American program constructed on the Ziller plan. The following is a citation: —

"The Jewish and German historical materials, which are made the moral-educative basis of the common school by the Herbartians, can be of no service to us except by way of example. Neither sacred nor German history can form any important part of an American course of study. Religious instruction has been delegated to the Church, and German history touches us indirectly, if at all. The epochs of history from which American schools must draw are chiefly those of the United States and Great Britain. France, Ger-

[1] *General Method*, pp. 47, 48.

many, Italy, and Greece may furnish some collateral matter, as the story of Tell, of Siegried, of Alaric and Ulysses, but the leading epochs must be those of our own national history.

" Has the English-speaking race of North America passed through a series of historical epochs which, on account of their moral-educative worth, deserve to stand in the center of the common school course ? Is this history adapted to cultivate the highest moral and intellectual qualities of children as they advance from year to year ? There are few if any single nations whose history could furnish a favorable answer to this question. The English in America began their career so late in the world's history, and with such advantages of previous European culture, that several of the earlier historical epochs are not represented in our country. But perhaps Great Britain and Europe will furnish the earlier links of a chain whose later links were firmly welded in America.

" The history of our country since the first settlements less than three hundred years ago is by far the best epitome of the world's progress in its later phases that the life of any nation presents. On reaching the new world the settlers began a hand-to-hand, tooth-and-nail conflict with hard conditions of climate, soil, and savage. The simple basis of physical existence had to be fought for on the hardest terms. The fact that everything had to be built up anew from small beginnings on a virgin soil gave an opportunity to trace the rise of institutions from their infancy in a Puritan dwelling or in a town meeting, till they spread and consolidated over a continent. In this short time the people have grown from little scattered settlements to a nation, have experienced an undreamed-of material expansion, have passed through a rapid succession of great political struggles, and have had an unrivalled evolution of agriculture, commerce, manufactures, inventions, education, and social life. All the elements of society, material, religious, political, and social, have started with the day of small things and have grown up together.

"There is little in our history to appeal to children below the fourth grade, that is, below ten years; but from the beginning of the fourth grade American history is rich in moral-educative materials of the best quality and suited to children. We are able to distinguish four principal epochs: 1. The age of pioneers, the ocean navigators like Columbus, Drake, and Magellan, and the explorers of the continent like Smith, Champlain, La Salle, and Fremont. 2. The period of settlements, of colonial history, and of French and Indian wars. 3. The Revolution and life under the Articles of Confederation till the adoption of the Constitution. 4. Self-government under the Union and the growth and strengthening of the federal idea. While drawing largely upon general history for a full and detailed treatment of a few important topics in each of these epochs we should make a still more abundant use of the *biographical* and *literary* materials furnished by each. The concentration of school studies, with a historical series suggested by the culture epochs as a basis, would utilize our American history, biography, and literature in a manner scarcely dreamed of heretofore.

"We shall attempt to illustrate briefly this concentration of studies about materials selected from one of the culture epochs. Take, for example, *the age of pioneers* from which to select historical subject-matter for children of the fourth and fifth grades. It comprehends the biographies of eminent navigators and explorers, pioneers on land and sea. It describes the important undertakings of Columbus, Magellan, Cabot, Raleigh, Drake, and others, who were daring leaders at the great period of maritime discovery. The pioneer explorers of New England and the other colonies bring out strongly marked characters in the preparatory stage of our earliest history. Smith, Champlain, Winthrop, Penn, Oglethorpe, Stuyvesant, and Washington are examples. In the Mississippi Valley De Soto, La Salle, Boone, Lincoln, and Robertson are types. Still farther west Lewis, and Clarke, and the pioneers of California, complete this historical epoch in a series of great enterprises.

"Most of them are pioneers in new regions beset with dangers of wild beasts, savages, and sickness. A few are settlers, the first to build cabins and take possession of the land that was still claimed by red men and still covered with forests. The men named were leaders of small bands sent out to explore rivers and forests, or to drive out hostile claimants at the point of the sword. Any one who has tried the effect of these stories upon children of the fourth grade will grant that they touch deep native interest. But this must be a genuine and permanent interest to be of educative value. The moral quality in this interest is its virtue. Standish, Boone, La Salle, and the rest were stalwart men whose courage was keenly and powerfully tempered. They were leaders of men by virtue of moral strength and superiority. Their deeds have the stamp of heroism, and in approving them the moral judgments of children are exercised upon known material. These men and stories constitute an epoch in civilization because they represent that state which just precedes the first form of settled society. In fact some of the stories fall in the transition stage, where men followed the plough and wielded the woodman's axe, or turned to the warpath as occasion required. In every part of the United States there has been such a period and something corresponding to it in other countries. We are prepared to assume, therefore, that these historical materials arouse a strong interest, implant moral ideas, and illustrate a typical epoch. These are also very real. These men, especially the land pioneers, were our own predecessors, traversing the same rivers, forests, and prairies where we now live and enjoy the fruits of their hardihood and labor." [1]

Following the outline of his historical material is a general scheme of concentration for remaining branches. Dr. McMurry has exemplified his theories by compiling two volumes of pioneer history stories, and preparing the first two numbers of a series of monographs on Special Methods.[2] His monograph on Geography is noteworthy from the fact of its full recognition

[1] *General Method*, pp. 95-98.

[2] *Special Methods*, (1) History and Literature, (2) Geography, also Pioneer Stories, Public School Publishing Co., Bloomington, Ill.

of the value of commercial geography in elementary education.

A bibliography at the close of this volume gives in detail most of the contributions that have thus far been made in the effort to adapt Herbartian ideas to American conditions.

CHAPTER II

THREE PLANS FOR THE CORRELATION OF STUDIES

THAT the rational articulation of studies is a pressing problem in American education cannot be doubted. It is a consummation everywhere demanded but nowhere achieved by the celebrated Report of the Committee of Ten on Secondary Education.[1] Why there is no coördination in this Report it is not difficult to see. Nine independent bodies of specialists meeting in different places and having no correspondence could not be expected to produce a course of study in which the various branches should be organically connected. Dr. Frick and his hundred or more associates upon *Lehrproben und Lehrgänge* worked upon the special branches for eight years before they ventured to offer an organic course of study. The problems arising from the attempt at rational articulation being so difficult, it would be a cause of astonishment, had these independent conferences been able by intuition to do at a stroke what can only be effected by much reflection and experiment. The central committee did not attempt to modify the reports of the specialists

[1] This Report, made to the National Council of Education in 1894, is published by the Bureau of Education, Washington, D.C.

except to the extent of diminishing the time demanded, so that a workable program might be obtained. But though the final work of coördination remains a pious wish so far as the Report is concerned, it must not be inferred that the conferences have made no progress in this direction. There has been an honest attempt to fix upon a rational selection and sequence of topics for each important study or group of studies. And it may easily be conceded that a rational unity of treatment for each branch is preferable to a crude, one-sided, or visionary concentration of all subjects. Furthermore, each important group of related subjects is justified in presenting its claim for its own principle of sequence, unless, indeed, according to Ziller, we grant that some subjects are so important that they form a Procrustean bed to which all others with conflicting principles of development must be fitted. If this claim is not admitted, it follows that most important progress has already been made toward the coördination of the studies of Secondary Schools.

That the importance of coördination is seen also in the department of Elementary Education may be inferred from the following questions put to hundreds of leading superintendents and teachers by the Committee of Fifteen from the Department of Superintendence of the National Educational Association : —

CORRELATION OF STUDIES

1. Should the elementary course be eight years, and the secondary course four years, as at present ? Or,

should the elementary course be six years and the secondary course six years ?

2. Has each of the grammar school studies — language (including reading, spelling, grammar, composition), mathematics (arithmetic, algebra, plane geometry), geography, history, natural science (botany, zoölogy, mineralogy), penmanship, drawing, etc., a distinct pedagogical value ? If so, what is it ?

3. Should other subjects than those enumerated in the second question, such as manual training (including sloyd, sewing, and cooking), physical culture, physics, music, physiology (including the effects of stimulants and narcotics), Latin, or a modern language, be taught in the elementary school course ? If so, why ?

4. Should the sequence of topics be determined by the logical development of the subject, or by the child's power to apperceive new ideas ? Or, to any extent by the evolutionary steps manifested by the race ? If so, by the evolution of the race to which the child belongs, or that of the human race ?

5. What should be the purpose of attempting a close correlation of studies ?

(a) To prevent duplication, eliminate non-essentials, and save time and effort ?

(b) To develop the apperceiving power of the mind ?

(c) To develop character ? A purely ethical purpose ?

6. Is it possible on any basis to correlate or unify all the studies of the elementary school ?

7. If not, may they be divided into two or more groups, those of each group being correlated ?

8. Is there any way of correlating the results of work in all the groups?

9. What should be the length of recitation periods in each year of the elementary school course? What considerations should determine the length?

10. In what year of the course should each of the subjects mentioned in questions 2 and 3 be introduced, if introduced at all?

11. In making a program, should time be assigned for each subject, or only for the groups of subjects suggested in question 7?

12. How many hours a week for how many years should be devoted to each subject, or each group of subjects?

13. What topics may be covered in each subject, or each group of subjects?

14. Should any subject, or group of subjects, be treated differently for pupils who leave school at 12, 13, or 14 years of age, and for those who are going to a high school?

15. Can any description be given of the best method of teaching each subject, or group of subjects, throughout the school course?

16. What considerations should determine the point at which the specialization of the work of teachers should begin?

17. On what principle should the promotion of pupils from grade to grade be determined? Who should make the determination?

Not only do we have these indications of the drift of thought in the National Educational Association, but we have Col. F. W. Parker's inspiring volume of 491 pages on the *Theory of Concentration*[1] — perhaps the most thoroughgoing and extensive work ever written upon this subject. Although Colonel Parker makes no claim of being a Herbartian, his theory of concentration reminds us strongly of Ziller's in its purpose of unifying all knowledge. The principle on which this is to be effected, however, is totally different from Ziller's. Like the Herbartians, he takes the strongest grounds against the idea of *formal discipline*, especially when sought through *form* studies alone, such as language, grammar, and mathematics. Actual, concrete knowledge of the same sort that has constituted the ante-school experience of the child, shall be the material through which all form is to be taught. In the center stands the child surrounded by *energy* working through *matter*. This matter is studied under the following heads: mineralogy, geology, geography, astronomy, meteorology, botany, zoölogy, anthropology, ethnology, history. This is a hierarchy of sciences, and each is to be taught in its relations to its fellows. *Universal law* is to be the principle of unification of knowledge in the mind of the child. Next, we have the modes of attention called observing, reading, hearing-language. Then come the modes of expression called gesture, writing, speech, drawing, painting, modelling, making, music. Lastly, we have the modes of Judgment — called form and number. Through the expression of concrete related knowledge (chiefly of the natural world, it would seem) we are to develop all needed skill in the use of forms. Formal studies as such should not be taught, for this is an inversion

[1] New York: E. L. Kellogg & Co., 1894.

of nature and a perversion of every sound educational theory. No group of subjects such as history and literature on the one hand, or natural science on the other, is to form the core about which the other subjects shall be concentrated and to whose principle of development the others shall be subordinated; but every subject shall have equal validity with every other, except that *thought* shall precede expression, the principle of unification or concentration being the rational, philosophical relation that exists by nature among the various departments of human knowledge. The following citation from pp. 27–8 illustrates this natural coördination: " The first definition of geography that I give is this: Geography is the knowledge or science of the present appearance of the earth's surface. This definition premises that there have been countless other appearances in past æons, that constant changes have been going on in the crust of the earth, and that changes will be continuously made in the future. The present appearance of the earth's surface is the result, or present effect, of countless changes in the earth's crust. Geologists teach us that the earth's creation is going on to-day in precisely the same way and by the same causes as it has been going on for countless ages. To know geography is to know the present appearance of the earth's surface. This definition gives geography a place as a branch of study and shows its relation to other studies. Any definition more comprehensive than this would include other subjects. Thus the study of the surface of the earth is a study by itself, excluding by its definition all other branches."

Concentration based on the philosophic unity of all knowledge is a distinctly American contribution to the theory of education. Some of its limitations will soon be pointed out.

We have before us two general plans of CONCENTRATION, Ziller's and Colonel Parker's, and one for coördination, that offered by Dr. Frick. Granting to each of the theories of concentration its strong points, it is still obvious that both have serious limitations, some of which may be mentioned: —

1. Ziller's scheme of concentration assumes, in the first place, that the past is always simpler, hence more interesting, to the child than the present, and that consequently the culture epochs are the invariable guide to sequence in the culture subjects. This assumption, notwithstanding the unquestioned advantage presented by a historical sequence, can hardly be successfully maintained as an invariable principle. To begin with, only the finest historians are able to make such a picture of past conditions of life that the child can have any adequate understanding of the events narrated in history. Pioneer life, in spite of its seeming simplicity, may be really complex to the young because of its poverty of the means now surrounding every child. Think of the devices and roundabout methods that had to be resorted to because of the limitations of the people in the means for transportation; for obtaining and cooking food; for erecting, heating, and lighting houses; for manufacturing clothing; for obtaining books, papers, magazines, works of art, and other means of culture. To portray the conditions under which ancient or for-

eign peoples wrought is a correspondingly difficult task.

Again, it may be that the elements for the explanation of even complicated social or material relations lie in the environment of the child, so that there is no need to go to the developments of history for an explanation. Suppose one wished to make a ten-year-old boy understand something of a self-binding harvester. One might indeed go back to the Book of Ruth for a lesson on the use of the hand-sickle, and then show the development into the scythe, then into the cradle, then the back and forth movement of the McCormick sickle, then the self-raker, the Marsh Harvester on which the binders rode, and finally the self-binder itself. But though this tracing of the historical evolution would be interesting and under some circumstances very valuable, it is not necessary to an understanding of the machine in question. Hand-sickles, scythes, and rakes are used for some purposes to-day. In fifteen minutes an instructor could illustrate the whole process with the elements at hand — the cutting of the grain, the use of the reel in place of the hand for holding the grain to be cut, the platform for carrying and elevating the grain instead of the old process of gathering into bundles, the binding by means of a steel arm and a twine, instead of the old method of binding with straw by hand, and finally the grouping of bundles into winrows for shocking. The elements necessary for explanation are right at hand, and for clearness need no excursion into historical epochs. In the same way, the elements for the proper comprehension of legal, social, governmental,

and economic organizations may all lie in the environment of the child, making it quite unnecessary to trace
their development from antiquity through the various
culture stages of the race.   Why, for illustration, cannot the modern German boy with his knowledge of
railroads, steamboats, and bridges; of gunpowder, cannon, and breech-loading rifles, understand the last war
with France, as well as the guerilla warfare waged
with antiquated weapons by his savage ancestors
against the legions of Rome ?   Is not the progress
through the culture epoch of more value as a stimulant
to the imagination, as a means for touching the fancy,
for enriching the social life, and for broadening the
sympathies than it is as a necessary means for understanding?   If this is the truth, then we must grant
to the environment of the child as great a value for
apperception as is contained in progress through culture
epochs, even for culture subjects.

   The second limitation to which Ziller's plan is subjected, is that it is a scheme for SUBORDINATION for most
branches, and not one of COÖRDINATION.   Non-culture
subjects, like the natural sciences, are compelled to
accept a principle of development not their own, provided they are so fortunate as to be granted any at all.
It is to incidental suggestions arising from history
and literature that the nature-subjects owe their appearance at any given point upon the program.   It
might perhaps be granted that, in the first years of
school life, when scientific sequence is a matter of
small moment, such a method for selecting nature-
topics is open to the least objection.   But if the study
of nature is to be seriously undertaken, it seems in-

evitable that, just as it has developed for itself the laboratory method of verification and inductive observation, releasing itself from the shackles of literary treatment, so too it must be granted a correlated sequence arising from its own constitution, not from that of subjects naturally alien to it.

2. Fascinating as Colonel Parker's scheme of concentration may appear at first sight, it involves two chief difficulties, one physical and the other psychical, together with any number of undesirable tendencies. The two great difficulties involved arise from the fact that to make the philosophical unity of knowledge the principle of concentration it is necessary to have an adult philosopher to teach and an infant philosopher to learn. It is a physical (and economic) impossibility to prepare two hundred thousand philosophers, more or less, to do the teaching; and it is a psychical impossibility to produce any infant philosophers to do the learning. Simple associations of facts children can make, but they can see no far-reaching unifying principles. To make them appear to do so leads to worse formalism than any we seek to avoid.

Among the undesirable tendencies of this plan the following may be mentioned: —

(1) There seems an undue emphasis upon the material facts of knowledge, and a corresponding neglect of the culture side. The topics in which inherent thought is to be developed are mineralogy, geology, geography, astronomy, meteorology, biology, zoölogy, anthropology, and history. How different from this is Ziller's emphasis of the culture subjects history, literature, and religion, which in his view are so important for the

spiritual and moral development of man that they are
worthy to be the core of study to which all form and
nature study should be subordinated. The savage,
even, learns much of nature, but his savagery exists
because he knows so little of man and his institutions.
The history of the world indicates that civilization has
been possible without natural science, but that it cannot exist without culture knowledge. Were we forced,
therefore, to abandon either in elementary education,
we should keep the culture and let the science go.
For this reason a scheme of concentration that appears
to lay such heavy stress upon the facts of the material
world is open to serious objection.

(2) Another practical difficulty at once arises when
the attempt is made to teach all modes of expression,
such as writing, speech, drawing, painting, modelling,
and making, incidentally, as the natural method of expressing the inherent thought gained in the knowledge
subjects. Such modes of expression as arise naturally
and inevitably in expressing thought may perhaps be
left to incidental care, but those that occasion great
mechanical and mental difficulties, like writing, drawing, spelling, etc., are in most cases likely to be neglected if taught incidentally. In the long run and
with the majority of teachers, what is incidental
comes to be regarded as unimportant, and suffers a
corresponding neglect.

(3) A philosophical unity of knowledge as a basis
for concentration leads inevitably to an emphasis of
the LOGICAL at the expense of the PSYCHOLOGICAL
principle of sequence. It is only after the separate
sciences are well developed individually that their

philosophical interrelations are clearly perceived. In making these late-seen interrelations the basis of concentration, the natural tendency would be to make the various sciences take the direction and sequence of topics indicated by their development as logically completed wholes. The apperception of the child is not scientific, however, but depends upon the limits and tendencies fixed by environment, experience, and childish tastes and fancies. The sequence of topics in knowledge must, therefore, be psychological before it is logical.

The only scheme of true coördination of studies furnished by the followers of Herbart is that offered by Dr. Frick. Its chief features are (1) that it places the present environment of the child at least on a par with the culture epochs as a guide to the selection and arrangement even of culture-studies; (2) that it allows the nature-studies to have their own principle of development so far as selection and sequence are concerned; (3) that it provides for the greatest possible unity in each important subject; (4) that it takes advantage of natural and simple relations existing among the studies, so arranging and presenting the various topics that these relations may appeal with full force to the child. In short, his plan is to depend upon simple associations among the ideas presented by instruction, leaving until the later stages of education all attempts to bring to view that unification of knowledge which comes through a grasp of underlying philosophical principles.

Like other Herbartians, Dr. Frick divides studies

into two groups — CULTURE- and NATURE-studies, each group having both *form* and *content* branches. Languages are, in general, the form side of culture-subjects, and mathematics the form side of nature-studies.

This classification has for the past half century been a good one, but a new spirit is coming into our civilization, which even if not yet recognized by the teacher will, however, soon force a recognition. Education has, in its elements, at least, now become universal, and the conditions of life for the masses are rapidly changing. We cannot multiply populations indefinitely without at the same time abandoning whole groups of old ideals in every important field of activity, education included.

Before the final chapter of this book can be written, setting forth the author's conception of a practicable principle of coördination of studies for English-speaking peoples, there must be an exposition of the new ideals that should follow from the new conditions of life. This exposition it is the business of the next chapter to set forth.

CHAPTER III

A NEW ERA IN EDUCATION

NOTHING is older than hostility to new ideas. When, in important aspects of life, they have tended to dominate large numbers of men, their christening has not unfrequently been a baptism of blood. This has been the history of religious and governmental changes.

Every significant proposition to abandon the beaten path of the fathers in whatever realm of thought is sharply challenged by many people both as to purpose and method. Not only is this true in Church and state, but it is equally true in education, which is at once a cause and a result of both.

To a large extent educational ideals arise from the conditions under which men worship their Creator, provide their food, and secure their civil liberty. But these conditions constantly change, sometimes rapidly, sometimes slowly, whereas our ideas of education are periodic, rather than constant in their corresponding advance. Our imaginations become completely adjusted to one set of conditions, so that we find it difficult if not impossible to readjust them to a new order of things. How slowly and reluctantly, for instance, have we reconstructed our religious imaginations to meet the truths revealed by the new astronomy, the science of geology, and the demonstrated portions of the theory of evolution! For 1350 years the development of the Christian religion had been side by side with the Ptolemaic theory of astronomy, in which the earth was the stationary center around which revolved sun, planets, and stars. What more natural than that Heaven should be above, and Hell below? But if the sun is to be the center, the image constructed by the imagination is distorted if not destroyed. Our youthful minds become adjusted to the literal Mosaic account of creation, but the imagination will not accord with the science of geology as we know it to-day. Our early conceptions of primeval life come into conflict with the idea of an orderly evolution. Slowly, reluctantly, and sometimes only in our children do we revise these old constructions of an active imagination to make them conform to demonstrated laws.

Belated ideals are more to be expected in education than in government and religion, for the antithesis between inherited educational conceptions and the new conditions under which men must work are not so sharply accented here as elsewhere. Men have ample freedom to follow their notions in the higher education of their children, so that they do not feel called upon to defend their educational faith as they do their faith in civil and church affairs. For this reason it often comes to pass that those who should be the leaders, become the retarders of educational thought, leaving the direction of it to practical men of the world, whose lives are in close touch with the economic activities of the present, and whose minds are not arrested by ideals that were the products of an older state of civilization.

Plato and Aristotle sought to get to the heart of the material world, to find the stuff of which things are made and the primal forces that produce them. Building upon the foundations laid by Aristotle, Thomas Aquinas and Duns Scotus sought to demonstrate to the understanding the truths of revelation, that is, to rationalize the Christian creed. Descartes and Kant have changed the basis, and instead of founding philosophy upon the lowly earth, or suspending it from the vaulted sky, they rest it upon the fundamental truths of human consciousness. The standpoint of philosophy has thus shifted from material to miracle and from miracle to mind, each stage summing up and including all that had gone before. Closely analogous to this movement has been that of education. The oldest yet perhaps the most common ideal of higher education to-day is that liberal training of the mind consists chiefly of ancient languages and mathematics. The entrance requirements of our colleges are mostly adjusted to this idea.

Vast indeed is the debt that civilization owes to these incomparable instruments of education. Once they were wholly adequate to the educational needs of the world. But should we forget that since the days when the classics obtained their ascendancy the world has become democratic, that higher education from being the privilege of a small class has become a necessity for the leaders of all classes? Shall we ignore the fact that at that time the mother-tongue of most countries was the vehicle of little or no learning? It was near the middle of the last century before Wolff first taught philosophy to speak German. Previous to that time Latin was the almost universal language of learned works. The rise and growth of science is almost within the memory of men now living, while the wonderful development of industrial enterprise, with its concentration of capital and organization of labor, is confined almost to the present century. In short, the classics took their rise when they were the only receptacles of knowledge, when no natural science existed, when industry was undeveloped, when education was the prerogative of priests and literati, and when the surging masses had not yet risen to assert for themselves the rights of man. Under these circumstances it is not strange that the imagination of the scholar should have constructed a picture of classical education in colors so bright that they still endure.

Mathematics won its prominent place in our curriculum largely through the brilliant results obtained by Newton and his contemporaries. To it chiefly we owe our modern scientific development. The latter half of our own century has seen the rise and perfection of the natural sciences as instruments of education. Taught at first by literary methods, they made but little impression, but during the last twenty-five years they have developed a method of their own — that of inductive research and verification in the laboratory. So vast have been the conquests of

science in our own times that a large part of our
educators have reconstructed their educational ideal,
yielding to science an honored place side by side with
the older linguistic branches.

The second grand movement in the history of education since the Renaissance has now taken place.
The first represents the supremacy of the humanities
in the form of ancient languages; the second, the admission of the natural sciences as coördinate branches.
To-day we are preparing to inaugurate a third and
grander period, which shall be in itself the synthesis
and final culmination of the other two.

Man, with only an introspective knowledge of himself, is what the mediæval monks thought him — a citizen of Heaven wretchedly stranded upon this desert
island in the sea of Eternity. This means for the
learned, alternating ecstasy and despair, and for the
masses, ignorance, poverty, disease, together with their
attendant forms of wretchedness. Universal education, high standard of living, and at the same time
dense population, are not to be thought of under such
conditions.

On the other hand, man can never know so much of
nature that he needs to know nothing of himself. In
a broad sense Pope's dictum, "The proper study of
mankind is man," is still true. Not man simply as
an introspective being, or man as smothered in the
dust of science, but man as a universal being whose
spiritual ends are realized through the means that
science puts at his command. The classics were the
beginning of modern education; natural science has
been the contribution of more modern times. Both

of these enriched and focussed on life are to form a new era in education, that which in a broad and liberal sense may be called economic. This term may be easily misconstrued to mean a narrow utilitarianism, a restricted physical aptitude and skill obtained by the perpetual iteration of mindless exercises. Such a conception of the function of education, however, is unworthy the times in which we live.

The economic culmination of the humanistic and the scientific sides of our training, broadly considered, means the conscious direction of thought, power, and knowledge to the ends they are designed to accomplish.

To see how this is possible, it is necessary to point out a current illusion, generated by the old classical education. Many teachers have long thought, and still think, that a liberal education consists not in mastering knowledge, but in developing power through the medium of grammar and pure mathematics, the idea being that if we can once develop the power, it may be applied, like a mechanical force, to any desired end. Reflection will show that this supposed formal discipline of the mind by two kinds of study is largely mythical, but that if properly directed they are rather rich and concrete as far as they go, being, however, exceedingly narrow in range. What is gained by this grammatical drill? A keen, discriminating knowledge of the laws of thinking, and a power to distinguish the most subtle phases of thought. Every page of the text abounds in concrete illustrations of the things the classicist is trying to learn. Any sentence may illustrate the use of the dative case, or the intri-

cacies of the subjunctive mood, and this process of
illustration and verification of the laws of language
goes on day after day, month after month, year after
year. Were natural science half so persistent in the
discovery and exemplification of her laws, she would
have new triumphs to boast. Latin and Greek may in
the same way be concrete and practical. Their seeming formality is due to their psychological character.
That alone is formal and abstract which is divorced
from the purpose it should serve. The same richness
and concreteness are found in pure mathematics, thousands of problems being solved to exemplify a few rules.
This explains to us the admirable results of classical
training for those whose future callings are largely
introspective in character, such as the preacher, the
teacher, the statesman, and even the physician. On
the other hand, the psychological or subjective outcome of such an education explains the instinctive
hostility that practical men of the world have long
manifested for this training. Instead of the old
maxim, " discipline first and knowledge afterwards,"
we must adopt the truer watchword, " discipline
through knowledge." The chief defect of the old
education is not that it is good for no practical purpose, but that it is for so many callings in life a
partial and one-sided preparation. For the professional man or woman it may be economic in the true
sense, since it has direct bearing on future occupation ; for all but the learned professions, however, it
may be subjective and esoteric ; it may leave the mind
steeped in the antiquated conceptions of by-gone ages,
which taken as stages in a progress would be valu-

able, but which as a substitute for the ruling ideas of to-day bear the same relation to developed truth that the child does to the man. In the words of the German Emperor, this age needs young Germans, young Englishmen, young Americans, not young Greeks and Romans.

The truth is, as has been intimated, the old education was practical and economic for a small class to whom a concrete introspective training was the best preparation for life. Our problem, however, is the education of all classes. The introduction of the natural sciences has immensely broadened the scope of the usefulness of modern education. But the conception is comparatively new that, not only can science minister to the wants of a new class of our population, but that by a proper adjustment of subject-matter and the employment of right methods of teaching, all minds can be trained, and at the same time be prepared for the best possible success in their several callings. The powers that we have can be trained through the knowledge we most need; as in the binocular microscope, trained mind and acquired knowledge are focussed in the economic activities of every calling in life. Is drawing less educative when applied to the plans for a mighty temple, than when sketching the bust of a Pallas Athene to adorn one of its niches? Is botany less noble when discovering the laws of plant organization and investigating the conditions of healthy growth, than it is when it leads the youth of our land into field and forest in order to gather and name the flowers? Are not chemistry and physics quite as interesting, instructive, and educative when developed to the point of their economic application, as they are when arrested at their abstract stages out of all felt relations to ultimate ends?

In addition to the old narrow curriculum of classics and pure mathematics we have on the humanistic side, the English language and literature, modern foreign languages, modern history, together with the study of the rise and development of constitutional government and other democratic institutions. On the side of science, we have the marvellous development of pure and applied mathematics, of chemistry and physics, besides the modern biological sciences, whose principle of evolution has given new life to every great interest of the human mind. Besides these two lines of study, enriched and fertilized as they are by application to practical ends, we have another large group of studies applicable to the economic activities in the narrower sense. They are such branches as manual training, industrial drawing, industrial art, civil, mechanical, and electrical engineering, and the still greater subjects, finance and administration, together with economics, or the study of the laws that govern the production, distribution, and consumption of wealth.

What have we to expect from the new spirit that is animating the educational world? Everything that education can contribute to the progress of civilization. Once the world was in the hands of the monks. We know their ideals and their deeds. For a hundred years it has been in the hands of the scientists. We know what they have done. They have made it possible for many more people to live much better; but at the same time they have also made it possible for a few men with large brains and great capital so to dominate the people that though prosperity and high standards of living may in some measure be within the reach of the masses, yet under adverse circumstances the most wholesale misery may result. The future, therefore, belongs neither to the humanist, nor to the scientist as such, but to both combined in the economist. The mental effort once lavished on the logic of the schoolmen, and now on the development of science, must in the future be set to work in solving the economic problems of life.

I have said that the human element, represented still in large measure by the classic languages, is an indispensable element in any comprehensive modern education. One of the prominent results of the old studies is the appreciation of the beautiful generated in the soul. Beauty, if not the religion of the Greek, was its invariable attendant, — beauty not as an adorner and sweetener of life, but beauty as an end. Thus in the words of Emerson : —

"Tell them, dear, if eyes were made for seeing,
  Then beauty is its own excuse for being."

One has, however, but to consider what has been accomplished in many new institutions of learning where industrial art is studied, to find that in this respect also there has been a new combination. Not only is weary toil sustained by the hope of ultimate rewards, but it is sweetened and illumined throughout its course by artistic ideals. Beauty, therefore, from being an idol before which we may bow, becomes a cheering spirit whose wand transforms drudgery into pleasing labor. Why should not every workman be an artist? A dinner-table with only potatoes and bread for food, and water for drink may still be the center of pleasing intercourse. It need not be a stall for feeding. The coarsest material can be made into becoming garments, humble homes may enjoy the gladness of beauty. All this is attained, not through the elimination of art as such, but by an application of it to common things. Knowledge, thought-power, artistic taste, are no longer isolated and held aloof from daily living, but are blended, harmonized, and utilized to make life more worth living.

At the beginning of Western civilization, under favorable climatic conditions and with the minority able to enslave the majority, it was not unfitting that art should become the supreme end for which the educational forces of the time were organized. This stage of society may fitly be symbolized by the Apollo Belvidere, the classic repose of whose well-rounded form suggests nothing of the modern spirit. The symmetrical limbs are made, not for work, but for entrancing the eye. The placid features betoken no moral struggle, no resolution to overcome difficulties; they indicate rather a being made for sensuous enjoyment, not for thinking or volition.

During the great middle period of our civilization, when men were busied with revelation and subjective analysis, educational agencies were directed to these ends. The symbol of those times is the Madonna. Her upward straining eyes proclaim the renunciation of earth, the aspiration for heaven. Sense and will are dissolved in religious sentiment.

The antique brings the god to earth, the mediæval translates the mortal to the skies, but the modern man uses his godlike powers to realize the heaven within himself. His symbol is Michael Angelo's statue of Moses, the man who works out the destiny of his race upon earth by means of his heaven-lent powers. On his brow there are written both thought and resolution. His rugged form, his starting tendons and swelling muscles betoken the man of action. His is the modern spirit that focusses thought, sense, and sentiment upon the vital problems encountered in realizing the will of God upon earth. It is to these ends that our modern education must be consciously organized. Unless the thinking forces of this country are turned from the subordinated ideals of the past to the vital ones of the present, hunger and economic servitude will cause the masses to change evolution into revolution as they have done before, when those who should have been their leaders became their masters.

We shall, as in the past, need the poet to solace the soul, and the artist to delight the eye, but most of all we shall need to have all the power of learning applied to the elevation of man. Like the whirring dynamos propelled by the hitherto unused power of Niagara, which loses no beauty in being useful, this new educational influence, brought to view by the necessities of an economic age, has begun to generate a life current, which in the fulness of time is destined to warm, to move, and to light the world.

CHAPTER IV

PROPOSED BASES FOR THE COÖRDINATION OF STUDIES

THE critique of the THREE PLANS FOR THE CORRE-
LATION OF STUDIES in Chapter II of Part III leads
inevitably to the conclusion that the *coördination* of
studies is greatly to be preferred to their *concentration,*
whether we consider culture-studies or nature-studies
as the center about which all other branches should be
arranged and to which they shall be subordinated, or
whether, with Colonel Parker, we accept universal
natural law as the guide to presentation. Coördination
allows each important subject, or group of subjects, to
have its own principle of development, contenting itself
with natural and easy associations in the lower grades,
and not attempting to give a philosophic grasp of the
highest unity of knowledge until the pupil is sufficiently
mature to comprehend this phase of thought. Furthermore, coördination permits us to present one subject at a time, thus relieving us from the need of
abandoning important studies to the hazard of incidental treatment. The same discussion leads, too, to
the conclusion that the historical principle of sequence,
though of unquestioned value, need not be followed

blindly, but that the environment of the child is just as potent an influence in his understanding and interest as any adaptation of culture epochs to his periods of development can be.

The discussion of *A New Era in Education* in the preceding chapter calls attention to a fact often forgotten by the teacher, viz., that the highest function of education is to fit the pupil for life, — not the esoteric life of the recluse or the dreamy idealist, but the life of the man of affairs, who takes an active part in all that pertains to human welfare and advancement. Such a man is not merely subjectively but also objectively moral; he is a good parent, a good citizen, an efficient man of business, who is able to advance his own interests through honest promotion of the interests of others. Too many of our educational ideals are mediæval in their origin; they take as their model some worn-out conception of culture, or they fix their gaze upon some special calling, forgetting that education is no longer the prerogative of the few professional classes, but has become the just privilege of all classes. If, then, we are in earnest about universal education, we must abandon these one-sided ideals, and, once for all, recognize that our education succeeds just to the extent that we make it focus upon the real activities of life. Rosenkranz is fond of emphasizing the idea of *self-estrangement* as a necessary means of culture. He says, "All culture, whatever may be its special purport, must pass through these two stages — of estrangement and its removal. Culture must intensify the distinction between the subject and the

object, or that of immediateness, though it has again
to absorb this distinction into itself; in this way the
union of the two may be more complete and lasting.
The subject recognizes, then, all the more certainly
that what at first appeared to it as a foreign existence
belongs to it potentially as its own possession, and
that it comes into actual possession of it by means of
culture."[1] This view, exaggerated it may be, is one
of the evils of modern education. The pupil is so
sunk in the distant, foreign, and alien, and submerged
for so long a time, that he often fails to come to himself at all, continuing to live in a land of dreams long
after he should have been in a land of realities. Whatever truth there may be in this theory is more safely
expressed by Herbart in his doctrine of *absorption* and
reflection, in which at one moment the pupil becomes
lost in the absorption of new experiences, but in the
next comes to himself, and makes the alien his own
through reflection. But these stages should not last
for long periods of time, as Rosenkranz implies they
may, for in that case the student is in danger of becoming a citizen of the alien land, and an adherent of
its dust-covered ideals.

For all these reasons, it is urged that modern
schools should distinctly recognize in their curricula
the presence of the economic idea, not only as a principle influencing the choice and pursuit of all knowledge, but also as a distinct center for an important
group of school activities. In addition, therefore, to
the traditional human and nature groups, we shall
need to add the third or economic group of studies.

[1] Rosenkranz, *Philosophy of Education*, pp. 27, 28.

Instead, therefore, of adopting Ziller's plan of using literature and history as a single core of concentration to which all other subjects shall be made subordinate, and from which they must derive their principle of sequence; or, on the other hand, of attempting a similar concentration about the nature-studies, the proposition is here made to have three coördinate, but more or less distinct cores or centers of unification, having constant cross-relations wherever the nature of the subject-matter and the convenience of the class-room make them advisable. Literature and geography assume the nature of universal correlating studies, since the concrete matter of all three cores has both literary and geographical aspects. The three cores appear as follows : —

1. The humanistic group of studies having a distinct ethical content in literature and history, and a historical development as seen in the culture epochs through which civilization has passed.

2. The nature group of studies having no specific ethical content and no long progression from primitive to higher and higher truths, since for the most part these studies have all been developed during the present century.

3. The third core represents the two factors man and nature in interaction, and is at once a principle of application for all studies, and a specific department, as seen in such subjects as manual training, industrial art, mechanical drawing, commercial geography, and the like.

Each of these groups must now be briefly discussed.

1. The Humanistic Core

However much the ultimate theories of education
may differ, it may fairly be asserted that in elementary education our best thinkers unite in the opinion
that concrete, interesting matter is far preferable to
the dry bones of purely formal and mechanical instruction. In place of the old motto of discipline *and*
knowledge, we have really adopted in practice the new
one, viz., discipline *through* knowledge. Furthermore,
the present almost universal interest in ethical training leads to the conclusion that our former standpoint
of mere intellectuality in school education is being
gradually shifted to one that takes far more cogni-
zance of the need of developing moral character.
From these facts it may be presumed that the proposition to make literature and history one core of unification, with which more formal linguistic studies
may be associated, will be received as seasonable and
practicable.

In the studies of this core, and with proper respect
to experience under modern conditions, Ziller's principle of following in the main the chief epochs of
civilization is a workable one. Literature should begin with the fable, which is of Asiatic origin, and
which presents the economic or utilitarian standpoint
of action. The fables represent virtuous action as
paying larger dividends of pleasure and advantage than
vice or wrong-doing. These should be accompanied by
folk-lore and fairy tales, which have taken their origin
in the primitive stages of society, and which intro-

duce moral ideas as ends of action. It should be noted that *modern* works on primitive life may be most admirable material, as, for instance, Longfellow's *Hiawatha;* the *content*, not the time of action or literary record, being the important thing. Following this stage, literature should show, in gradually broadening relations, the chief situations in which the individual may stand to organized society. Besides the literature already described we have also a literature of nature, and to some extent of economic life. An illustration is found in Robinson Crusoe, which, according to Ziller's plan, is taught in the second grade ostensibly as the center of the ethical group, whereas it is not essentially ethical, but economical. It develops in reality the industrial instincts of the child, while the ethical element is dragged in or magnified out of due proportion in order to fit an artificial scheme of coördination. The effort to attach a moral to those things not inherently moral in their nature is harmful rather than beneficial; character is not promoted by perpetual tinkering on the part of the teacher. Alongside of this ideal presentation of human acts and its results should stand the historical, and by following a like principle there will be no serious difficulty about unification. Early history will, as recommended by the Report of the Committee of Ten, begin with mythology, which will easily blend with the early literature, and will proceed to biography, which will assume largely the literary coloring in the mind of the child. This will gradually merge into history proper in the upper grammar grades.

Human deeds, both actual and ideal, are the expression of ethical forces, but language is necessary for their preservation and transmission. Language study becomes, therefore, merely the formal part of literary and historical study. In the elementary grades it is the mother-tongue that we must deal with, so that a sufficiently close coördination with these studies may be brought about. Were instruction in this branch of elementary education nothing more than lessons in composition, spelling, and penmanship, it might be made purely incidental to the other work. This is, however, not the case. The mother-tongue has a system of grammatical forms which represent the method of Anglo-Saxon thought. To master these forms is to be able to perceive the thought distinctions they represent. The approach to a perception of these distinctions, or grammatical ideas, must be slow, and to the child almost unconscious. By means of carefully graded concrete language exercises whose content shall be taken from the material of literature, history, and nature study, it is possible to make an easy approach to English grammar. Nearly all the material for composition-work proper may likewise be chosen from the same sources.

According to the view here presented, the literary and historical treatment of men, both in their individual and in their corporate or institutional capacity, together with the literary aspects of nature, are, in large degree, fitted to reveal to the child the moral order of the world in which he must live. They form, therefore, the most natural core for direct efforts to impart moral ideals and to inculcate right moral disposition.

2. The Scientific Core

In the case of nature-studies, the leading purpose and unifying principle must be presumed to be scientific rather than ethical in the narrower sense of the term. That it may be clearly understood in what sense science is and is not ethical, we should clearly distinguish between an ethical instrument and an ethical content. It is quite possible to give a boy a training in science that shall be ethical in a high degree, since he may be taught to be careful, diligent, painstaking, and truthful in all his mental operations. Blacking boots or sawing wood might also yield the same ethical lessons, yet we should not ascribe ethical content to the blacking, the brush, the wood-pile, or the saw. It is the boy's action that has the ethical quality, and in this case the things used are only the instruments of an ethical deed. In the same way science studies have a high value as instruments in the training of character, but since their content is scientific, material fact, having no quality of good or bad will, they certainly are morally quite indifferent. Whereas, then, the content of literature and history is ethical, since these exhibit the good or bad will of men, the content of nature-studies is in the last analysis non-ethical or scientific, since it pertains solely to the facts and laws of nature.

For reasons already given it is clear that the historical principle has little or no applicability to this group of subjects. We must therefore find other and more practicable bases for unification. It can hardly be said that scientists themselves are a unit as to what should constitute the proper selection, sequence, and correlation of topics in nature-studies; indeed, not very much thought has been given to the subject. Twenty years ago teachers were declaring that science has small value for education or discipline in any field. Its knowledge value was conceded, but since nearly all sought to teach it in accordance with the methods common in languages, mathematics, and philosophy, its own peculiar excellence as an instrument in education did not appear. In the higher education all this has been changed, so that science is now valued by liberal-minded men as much for its educational discipline as for its useful information. Science has become a clear exemplification of the principle of discipline *through* knowledge. The most, perhaps, that we can claim regarding nature-studies in elementary grades is that men are now ready to grant the priority of psychological grounds in sequence of parts and coördination of branches. The tendency has been to a tandem arrangement of subjects and a logical sequence of parts. This position has been, or is destined to be, abandoned. The environment of the child, his psychological needs, and the opportunities of season and situation, must determine in large measure the selection of material in the earlier grades. The Report of the Committee of Ten is rich in suggestions as to the selection and sequence of topics, though for reasons already given little or no coördination has been accomplished

Just as language constitutes the formal aspect of humanistic studies, on the one hand, so mathematics is the formal aspect of nature-study in its quantitative relations, on the other. Hitherto our elementary work in number has been largely divorced from any considerable concrete matter and taught chiefly as an abstraction. While nothing can make mathematics easier than it is by nature, much can make it easier and more interesting than it has been in practice. Professor Jackman points out that about the only concrete matter we have used has been the idea of value, while Colonel Parker, in his *Theory of Concentration*, shows very clearly how numerical calculations may be associated with distances, areas, volumes, weights, densities, and sizes, to say nothing of time and forces.[1] The chief reason, perhaps, why so many arithmetics limit their concrete illustrations of numerical relations to considerations of value, is that heretofore so few content studies have been taught in the school. With their advent, however, arithmetic need no longer stand as an unrelated part of the curriculum.

It appears evident that number and culture subjects are practically incommensurable, beyond the barest beginnings of numerical relations. Three persons may be mentioned in a story, and it is not absurd that the primary teacher should use this fact to verify the idea of the number involved. Yet, at the most, this helps merely to associate number with objects. Any attempt to establish important numerical relations by means of such material would be far-fetched and ineffective. The case is different, however, with natural science and with economic and business affairs. Here quantitative relations force themselves upon us,

[1] *Theory of Concentration*, Chapter IV.

being often essential to complete comprehension of a subject. It is for these reasons that attempts to correlate mathematics with literature and history seem fantastic, while efforts to do the same with the sciences as well as with economic values appear natural and rational.

3. The Economic Core

The third core of instruction, here called the economic, has been but partially recognized in our course of study. It is the purpose of the preceding chapter to show how significant for the welfare and progress of mankind this phase of education is. A child not trained for the social and economic environment in which he must live is by no means rightly educated. Should we insist upon clothing the inhabitants of warm countries with bear skins, and upon feeding them with blubber, we should commit no greater breach of the eternal fitness of things, than we may now easily commit by failing to adapt the child's education to the needs of modern life. Universal formal education into the years of manhood as a basis for the special preparation for callings is a schoolmaster's dream, unattainable even if desirable, and undesirable even if attainable. Education must fit for living, all along the line, and the better it is adapted to this end the more the people will cherish and promote it.

The economic trend of education must be observed both as a *principle* for all study, and as a *department* of special work. As a principle, it seeks to focus all instruction upon the practical ends it should serve.

As a department, it has a double aspect, the adaptation of nature to man, and the preparation of man for his conquest over nature. There are, accordingly, two phases of its appearance in the curriculum. The first is the direct physical training the child needs for mastering and utilizing the forces of nature; and the other is the more contemplative study of economic manifestations, such as are seen in industries, commerce, agriculture, and the like. The first of these two sides is the very important practical education now known in the elementary schools as manual or industrial training, and the second is the view brought to light through economic and social literature, reinforced by the commercial and social aspects of geography.

Many manuals describing the sequence and conduct of manual training work of all grades have been published. The principle of sequence depends for the most part upon psychological and practical grounds. It is evident that no sequence, however philosophical in itself, can be adopted that plainly transcends the capacity of the schools with respect to teachers, materials, and appliances.

But little serious attempt has been made to select a body of literature to stimulate in the mind an interest in the correlation between man and nature, and in fact it is only in very recent times that a literature has begun to grow up that takes full account of modern economic and social environments. *Robinson Crusoe* is a classic upon the imaginative treatment of industrial evolution. Robinson Crusoe's constant thought is how he shall preserve his life and add to his comfort by mastering nature with the slender means at his command. The surest evidence of the economic trend of this work is that most children are at once stimulated by their reading of *Robinson Crusoe* to dig caves, and to construct boats, pottery, huts and the like, the ethical element remaining mostly in the background. The greatest obstacle to the use of this book in the schools has been its labored style, its heavy vocabulary, and its introspective analyses. A carefully edited edition has now been prepared for the use of pupils in the third and fourth grades.[1] More advanced imaginative literature of this type may be found in Jules Verne's books, the *Swiss Family Robinson*, More's *Utopia, The House that Jack Built*, Lawrence's *Adventures among the Glass Blowers*, Rutledge's *Every Boy's Book*, and the like. A literature fitted to the modern conditions of social and family life is also growing up, a type of which may be seen in the books of Louisa M. Alcott for children.

Just as language is the formal side of the ethical core, and mathematics of the scientific, so mechanical drawing is the formal side of manual training and industrial art, with which it may be closely associated.

We have now three parallel-lying and somewhat independent cores of unification about which closely related subjects are grouped. The chief idea of the first, taken in a broad sense, is ethical, representing the deeds of man as a free being, the principle of sequence being to considerable extent the historical; the spirit of the second group is scientific, not ethical,

[1] *Robinson Crusoe*, edited by Mrs. Lida B. McMurry, Public School Publishing Co., Bloomington, Ill.

and it represents nature in its independent aspects, the principles of sequence and correlation being determined chiefly by psychological grounds and outward circumstances, and only secondarily by the logical order of developed sciences; the third core of unification represents man and nature in interaction, and lays the chief emphasis upon preparing the child through industrial training the better to master and direct the forces of nature, providing at the same time a literary or imaginative contemplation of the economic field, and also a study of actual conditions in commercial geography.

Before concluding, it may be well to add a few practical considerations regarding special means for coördinating the various subjects of the curriculum. We have already seen how the reading in the form of literature pertains alike to culture, nature, and economics. It becomes, therefore, a possible means for bringing about close associations among the various realms of knowledge. The most universal content subject, however, is perhaps geography, whose manifold relations to the subject-matter of the curriculum may be briefly considered.

Heretofore geography seems to have been taught mostly from the political standpoint; that is, it has been used to show the present resultant of all the historical forces; but our conception of the function of geography is at once broadened when we look to it for a partial answer as to how the facts of political geography have come to be as they are. In other words, while we study the processes of history we look to physical geography to show us the conditions and determining natural forces that have brought results to pass. This aspect of geographical science is forced upon us in a measure when we consider such events as Napoleon's disastrous Moscow campaign, but history as often taught is as unconnected with the earth as if all its events took place in the upper air. Since history must have a place in which to unfold, and the unfolding itself is largely dependent upon the physical features of the country — its mountains, rivers, sea-coasts, forests, and climate, we have an explanation of the fact that geography, as the physical basis of history, is now becoming an important study in the curriculum. The elementary aspects of this relation should appear in the teaching of history and geography in the grammar schools.

Geography has also the most intimate connection with the biological sciences, since conditions of soil, climate, elevation, and contour determine the character and extent of the flora of a country. At the same time they determine the food supply of animals, thus forming the main condition for their multiplication, distribution, and migration. In other words, whereas science treats of plants and animals as individual things, we find in geography the chief external conditions of this existence in its manifold variations. To no small extent, furthermore, do we find in physical geography a support for other phases of science study.

Finally, what is perhaps one of the most important fields of geography has been almost wholly neglected in the schools, viz., commercial geography. This

shows in a remarkable way the interaction of the
two factors, man and nature, and forms an important
function in the economic education of the child. The
foundations for this study are easily and fairly laid
in the early home geography. While the child is out
of doors gathering the elements of his geographical
concepts, he may at the same time study the forms
of industry at his doors, even if it be no more than
the industry of the farm. A line of questions as to
what is produced in the neighborhood and what becomes of the product, what is received in return for
it, will open up a new world to the child. Then when
he comes to study the productions of other lands and
the geographical conditions that make them possible,
following this up by an investigation of the means
whereby the productions of one land may be exchanged
for those of another, he not only gets an enlarged
conception of his own place and function in the
world, but he learns practically the great ethical
lesson that every part of the world, and every man
in every part, is trying to serve self through service
to others.

The coördinating value of home and commercial
geography is admirably developed up to the fifth
grade of the elementary school in Dr. C. A. McMurry's
manual of *Special Methods in Geography*.[1]

The specific detail-work of correlating a curriculum
of study must be done, for the most part, in the
school itself. The effort to do this is most stimulating to all the teachers engaged in the effort.

[1] *Special Methods in Geography*, Dr. Chas. A. McMurry, Public
School Publishing Co., Bloomington, Ill.

Upon the basis already laid down, and with the example of such men as Ziller and Frick, each superintendent of schools will find the way open, not only to the immediate improvement of his schools, but to the invigorating of his whole corps of teachers.

APPENDIX

BIBLIOGRAPHY OF HERBARTIAN LITERATURE[1]

GENERAL PEDAGOGICS

Ackermann, Formale Bildung. *Langensalza.*

Ackermann, Pädagogische Fragen. 2d series. *Dresden.*

Frick-Meier, Sammlung pädag. Abhandlungen. *Halle.*

Herbart, Pädagogische Schriften, hrsg. v. Willmann. 2 vols. *Leipzig.*

Kern, Grundriss der Pädagogik. 4th ed. *Berlin*, 1887.

Lindner, Encyklopäd. Handbuch der Erziehungskunde. *Vienna*, 1884.

Rein, Pädagog. Studien ; alte Folge. 2 vols. *Vienna.*

Schiller, Handbuch der prakt. Pädagogik. 2d ed. *Leipzig*, 1889.

Stoy, Encyklopädie der Pädagogik. 2d ed. *Leipzig*, 1878.

Strümpell, Psychologische Pädagogik. *Leipzig*, 1880.

Strumpell, Das System der Pädagogik Herbarts. *Leipzig*, 1894.

Waitz, Allgem. Pädagogik, hrsg. v. Willmann. 3d ed. *Brunswick.*

Willmann, Didaktik. 2 vols. *Braunschweig*, 1882–89.

Ziller, Einleitung in die allg. Pädagogik. *Leipzig*, 1856. Allg. Pädagogik. 3d ed., hrsg. v. Just. *Leipzig.*

Ziller-Vogt, Jahrbücher des Vereins für wissenschaftliche Pädagogik. 24 vols. *Dresden.*

[1] From Van Liew's Translation of Rein's *Outlines of Pedagogics.*

I. PRACTICAL PEDAGOGICS

(A) THE FORMS OF EDUCATION

1. HOME PEDAGOGICS

Ackermann, Die häusliche Erziehung. *Langensalza,* 1888.
Stoy, Hauspädagogik. *Leipzig,* 1855.
Trüper, Die Familienrechte an der Erziehung. 2d ed. *Langensalza,* 1892.

2. SPECIAL EDUCATIONAL INSTITUTIONS

Education of the Deaf and Dumb

Oehlwein, Meine Erfahrungen u. Ansichten über das Wesen der Vier- und schwachsinnigen, etc. *Weimar,* 1883.

3. SCHOOL EDUCATION

(a) *The People's Schools*

Dörpfeld, Zwei pädagogische Gutachten. *Gütersloh,* 1877.
Leutz, Lehrbuch der Erziehung und des Unterrichts. 2d ed. *Tauberbischofsheim,* 1887.
Ranitzsch, Der Unterricht in der Volksschule. *Weimar,* 1888.

(b) *The Middle Schools (Burgher and Real-Schools)*

Dörpfeld, Der Mittelstand und die Mittelschule. *Barmen,* 1853.
Mager, Die deutsche Bürgerschule 1840.   Ed. by Eberhardt. *Langensalza.*
Otto, Der deutsche Bürgerstand und die deutsche Bürgerschule. *Leipzig,* 1871.
G. Wiget, Theorie und Praxis des Realschulunterrichts. *St. Gallen,* 1889.

(c) *Gymnasium*

Frick-Meier, Lehrproben und Lehrgänge. *Halle.*
Kern-H. J. Müller, Zeitschrift für das Gymnasialwesen. *Berlin.*
Schiller, Handbuch der prakt. Pädagogik. 2d ed. *Leipzig,* 1889.

(d) Girls' Schools

H. Grosse, Zur Reform des höh. Mädchenschulwesens, in :
  Richter, Der prakt. Schulmann, vol. 37, 1888. *Leipzig.*
Krusche, Uebersicht der Litteratur über weibliche Erziehung
  und Bildung in Deutschland von 1700-1886. *Leipzig,*
  1887.

(B) School Administration

1. School Legislation

Barth, Die Reform der Gesellchaft durch Neubelebung des
  Gemeindewesens. *Leipzig,* 1885.
Dörpfeld, Die freie Schulgemeinde und ihre Anstalten auf dem
  Boden der freien Kirche im freien Staate. *Gütersloh,*
  1863.
Dörpfeld, Die drei Grundgebrechen der hergebrachten Schulver-
  fassungen, etc. *Elberfeld,* 1869.
Dörpfeld, Ein Beitrag der Leidensgeschichte der Volksschule
  nebst Vorschlägen zur Reform der Schulverwaltung.
  2d ed. *Barmen,* 1883.
Dörpfeld, Das Fundamentstück einer gerechten, gesunden,
  freien und friedlichen Schulverfassung. *Hilchenbach,*
  1892.
Herbart, Ueber, Erziehung unter öffentlicher Mitwirkung. 1810.
Mager, Pädagog. Revue. VI. — XVII. Band ; XIX. Band.
  (Bruchstücke aus einer deutschen Scholastik.)
Mager, Die deutsche Bürgerschule.
  (Ed. by Eberhardt, *Langensalza.*)
Rein, Zur Schulgesetzgebung. Deutsche Rundschau. April No.
  1892. (Comp. Grenzboten : Erziehung und Sozialis-
  mus. No. 24, 1891.
Rolle, Die Selbständigkeit der Schule inmitten von Staat und
  Kirche : Pädag. Studien of Rein, 1889. No. 4.
Trüper, Die Familienrechte an der öffentlichen Erziehung. 2d
  ed. *Langensalza,* 1892.
Trüper, Die Schule und die sozialen Fragen unserer Zeit. 3
  Nos. *Gütersloh,* 1890.

2. Equipment of Schools

Piltz, Thüring. Schulmuseum. *Jena.*

3. Supervision of Schools

Dörpfeld, Leidensgeschichte der Volksschule. 2d ed. *Barmen,* 1882.

4. Preparation of Teachers

(a) *Seminaries for Teachers in the People's Schools*

Andreä, Zur inneren Entwicklungsgeschichte der deutschen Lehrerbildungsanstalten. *Kaiserslautern,* 1890–91 to 1891–92.

Rein, Ueber die Organisation der Lehrerbildung in Deutschland. Pädagog. Studien, 1881. 4th No. *Dresden.*

Stoy, Organisation des Lehrerseminars. *Leipzig,* 1869.

(b) *University-Seminaries*

Brzoska, Die Notwendigkeit pädagog. Seminare auf der Universität und ihre zweckmäszige Einrichtung. 2d ed. by Rein. *Leipzig,* 1887.
    (For Bibliography *v.* p. 205 *sqq.*)

Frick, Seminar. praeceptorum. *Halle,* 1883.

Rein, Ueber pädagog. Universitäts-Seminare. Neue d. Schule, 4–5 Nos.

Rein, Die Ausbildung für d. Lehramt an höher. Schulen, Grenzboten, 1890. 8th No.

Rein, Aus dem Päd. Univers.-Seminare zu Jena. Nos. 1–4. *Langensalza.*

Von Sallwürk, Das Staatsseminar. *Gotha,* 1890.

Schiller, Pädagog. Seminarien f. d. höh. Lehramt. *Leipzig,* 1890.

Vogt, Das pädagog. Universitäts-Seminar. *Leipzig,* 1884.

Zange, Gymnasial-Seminare und die pädagog. Ausbildung der Kandidaten des höh. Schulamts. 5th No. by Frick-Meyer: Sammlung pädagog. Abhandlungen. *Halle,* 1890.

II. THEORETICAL PEDAGOGICS

(A) The Fundamental Sciences of Pedagogics

I. Ethics

Flügel, Das Ich und die sittlichen Ideen im Leben der Völker, 2d ed. *Langensalza.*

Flügel, Die Sittenlehre Jesu. 2d ed. *Langensalza.*

Hartenstein, Die Grundbegriffe der eth. Wissensch. *Leipzig,* 1844.

Herbart, Allgem. prakt. Philosophie. Ed. by Hartenstein, vol. 8; Gesamtausgabe, by Kehrbach, vol. 4. *Langensalza.*

Nahlowsky, Praktische Philosophie. 2d ed. *Leipzig,* 1885.

Steinthal, Allgem. Ethik. *Berlin,* 1885.

Ziller, Allgem. philos. Ethik. 2d ed. *Langensalza,* 1886.

II. Psychology

Ballauff, Die Grundlehren der Psychologie. 2d ed. *Cöthen,* 1890.

Dörpfeld, Denken und Gedächtnis. 3d ed. *Gütersloh.*

Drobisch, Emp. Psychologie. *Leipzig,* 1843.

Flügel, Die Seelenfrage. 2d ed. *Cöthen,* 1884.

Hartmann, Die Analyse des kindl. Gedankenkreises. *Annaberg,* 1885.

Lange, Ueber Apprezeption. 4th ed. *Plauen. See* English References, page 198.

Lazarus, Das Leben der Seele. 3d ed. *Berlin.*

Lukens, Die Vorstellungsreihen u. ihre pädagog. Bedeutung. *Gütersloh,* 1892.

Männel, Ueber Abstraktion. *Gütersloh.*

Nahlowsky, Das Gefühlsleben. 2d ed. *Leipzig,* 1884.

Schoel, J. Fr., Herbarts philos. Lehre von der Religion. *Dresden,* 1884.

Strümpell, Gedanken über Religion u. relig. Probleme. *Leipzig,* 1888.

Volkmann, Lehrbuch der Psychologie. 3d ed. *Cöthen.*

(B) Aid-Science of Pedagogics : Physiology

(*A*) Teleology (*see* Ethics)

(*B*) Methodology (*see* Psychology)

I. General Didactics

Dörpfeld, Der didakt. Materialismus. 2d ed. *Gütersloh.*
Dörpfeld, Grundlinien einer Theorie des Lehrplans. *Gütersloh.*
Willmann, Didaktik als Bildungslehre. 2 vols. *Brunswick,*
1889.
Willmann, Pädagog. Vorträge. 2d ed. *Leipzig,* 1886.
Ziller, Grundlegung zur Lehre vom erz. Unterricht. 2d ed. by
Vogt. *Leipzig,* 1884.

1. Aims of Instruction

Grössler, Das vielseitige Interesse. *Eisleben,* 1883.
Vieth, Darf vielseitiges Interesse als Unterrichtsziel hingestellt
werden ? *Rogasen,* 1886.
Walsemann, Das Interesse. *Hanover,* 1884.

2. Means of Instruction

(*a*) *Choice of Material*

Rein, Gesinnungsunt. und Kulturgeschichte : Pädagog. Studien
1888. 2d No. *Dresden.*
v. Sallwürck, Gesinnungsunt. u. Kulturgeschichte. *Langensalza,*
1887.

(*b*) *Connection of Branches*

Ackermann, Ueber Konzentration : Pädag. Fragen, 1st series,
Dresden.
Dörpfeld, Zwei dringl. Reformen im Real und Sprachunt.
Gütersloh, 1883.
Loos, Der österr. Gymnasiallehrplan im Lichte der Konzentra-
tion. *Vienna,* 1892.
Merian-Genast, Ausführungen zum Lehrplan. *Jena,* 1892.

Rein, Pickel, Scheller, Theorie u. Praxis. 1st vol. 4th ed.
 Leipzig.
Willmann, Päd. Vorträge. 2d ed. *Leipzig.*

(c) *Treatment of Material*

Gleichmann, Ueber Herbart's Lehre von den formalen Stufen.
 2d ed. *Langensalza,* 1892.
Reich, Die Theorie der Formalstufen. *Langensalza,* 1889.
Th. Wiget, Die formalen Stufen. 4th ed. *Chur,* 1892.

II. Special Didactics

Frick-Meier, Lehrproben und Lehrgänge. *Halle.*
Jahrbücher des Vereins für w. Pädagogik. *Dresden.*
Rein, Pickel, Scheller, Theorie und Praxis des Volksschulunter.
 richts, etc. Vols. i.–viii. 4th ed. *Leipzig.*
Schiller, Handbuch der prakt. Pädagogik. 2d ed. *Leipzig.*
Ziller-Bergner, Materialien zur spez. Pädagogik. *Dresden,* 1886.

1. Instruction in Religion

Dörpfeld, Ein christl.-pädag. Protest. *Gütersloh,* 1869.
Reukauf, Philos. Begründung des Lehrplans des ev. Rel.-Unt.
 an höh. Schulen. *Langensalza,* 1892.
Staude, Präparationen zu den bibl. Gesch. des alten und neuen
 Testaments. 3 vols. 5th ed. *Dresden.*
Thrändorf, Die Behandlung des Religionsunterrichts. *Langen-
 salza,* 1887.
Thrändorf, Kirchengeschichtl. Lesebuch. *Dresden,* 1888.
Thrändorf, Der Religionsunterricht. (Präparationen.) *Dres-
 den,* 1890.

2. History

Dörpfeld, Repetitorium der Gesellschaftskunde und Begleitwort.
 2d ed. *Gütersloh,* 1890.
Eberhardt, Ueber Gesch.-Unt. Pädag. Studien. 4th No. *Vienna.*
Staude-Göpfert, Präparationen zur deutschen Geschichte. *Dres-
 den,* 1890.
Willmann, Der elem. Gesch.-Unt. *Leipzig,* 1872.

Wohlrabe, Präparationen zu profangesch. Quellenstoffen. *Gotha,* 1887.

Zillig, Der Geschichtsunt.   XIV. Jahrbuch d. Vereins f. w. Pädagogik.

3. DRAWING

Menard, Der Zeichenunterricht.   *Neuwied.*

Otto-Rein, Pädagog. Zeichenlehre.   3d ed.   *Weimar,* 1885.

Rein, Geschichte des Zeichenunt.   2d ed.   *Gotha,* 1889.

Rein, Der Zeichenunterricht im Gymnasium.   *Hanover,* 1889.

4. SINGING

Helm, Gesangunterricht in "Theorie und Praxis." Vols. i–viii. *Leipzig.*

5. INSTRUCTION IN LANGUAGE

Mager, Die genet. Methode des schulmässigen Unterrichts in fremden Sprachen und Litteraturen. 3d ed. *Zürich,* 1846.

Mager, Moderne Humanitätsstudien. 3 Nos. *Zürich.*

(a) German

Bliedner, Schillerlesebuch.   *Dresden.*

Eberhardt, Die Poesie in der Volksschule. 3 vols., 3d ed. *Langensalza,* 1886.

Stoy, Der deutsche Sprachunt.   3d ed.   *Vienna,* 1868.

(b) Other Foreign Languages

Bätgen, Zur Neugestaltung des franzos. Unt.   *Eisenach,* 1886.

Günther, Der Lateinunt. XIII. Jahrbuch d. V. f. w. Päd. *Dresden.*

6. GEOGRAPHY

Heiland, Das geographische Zeichnen.   *Dresden,* 1887.

Matzat, Methodik des geogr. Unt.   *Berlin,* 1886.

7. Natural Sciences

Beyer, Die Naturwissenschaften in der Erziehungsschule. *Leipzig*, 1885.

Conrad, Präparationen f. d. Physik-Unterricht. *Dresden*, 1889.

Dörpfeld, Repetitor. d. naturkundl u. humanist. Unt. 3d ed. *Gütersloh.*

Schleichert, Anleitg. zu botan. Beobachtungen, etc. *Langensalza*, 1891.

8. Mathematics

Falke, Propädeutik der Geometrie. *Leipzig*, 1869.

Fresenius, Die psycholog. Grundlagen der Raumwissenschaft. *Wiesbaden*, 1868.

Fresenius, Raumlehre. *Frankfurt*, 1861.

Hartmann, Handbuch des Rechenunterrichts. *Hildburghausen*, 1889.

Pickel, Die Geometrie der Volksschule. 16th ed. *Dresden.*

9. Manual Training

Barth-Niederley, Des d. Knaben Handwerkbuch. 5th ed. *Leipzig*, 1882.

Barth-Niederley, Die Schülerwerkstatt. *Leipzig*, 1882.

10. Turning

Hausmann, Das Turnen in der Volksschule. 4th ed. *Weimar.*

THEORY OF GUIDANCE

1. Training

Barth, Ueber den Umgang. 3d ed. *Langensalza.*

Kindergottesdienst, Ev. Schulbl. von Dörpfeld, 1887 u. 1888; Erziehungsschule von Barth. II., 9.

Scholz, Schulreisen. Aus dem pädagog. Universitäts-Seminar. 3d No. *Langensalza*, 1890.

Strümpell, Die pädag. Pathologie. *Leipzig*, 1890.

2. Government of Children

Nahlowsky, Ueber Herbarts reformator. Beruf. Zeitschrift f. exakte Philosophie, VII., 391–97.

Rein, Regierung, Unterricht u. Zucht. Pädag. Studien. 1st No. 3d ed. *Vienna.*

Stoy, Haus- und Schulpolizei. *Berlin*, 1856.

Ziller, Regierung der Kinder. *Leipzig*, 1857.

THE ENGLISH LITERATURE ON THE HERBARTIAN SYSTEM

THE following references contain most of what has been written in English upon the subject of the Herbartian pedagogics.   No attempt has been made to refer to works outside of this field.   The English-speaking teacher will, of course, have a more or less thorough acquaintance with the already extensive English literature on the subject of Pedagogy in general.   He has but to refer to such sources as the *Bibliography of Education* (*Boston*, 1886), by G. S. Hall and J. M. Mansfield, and the "Bibliography of Pedagogy" in Sonnenschein's *Cyclopedia of Education* (3d ed. 1892), to obtain the most comprehensive and accurate directions to the literature of every possible department of education, or to Dr. W. T. Harris's *Teachers' Course of Professional Reading for Home Work and Reading Circles*, for a general, profitable course of reading.   The following list will be of service to those who desire to become more familiar with the rising Herbartian views : —

Brown, G. P.: What is Interest ? in *Public School Journal*, vol. xii., No. 1., *Bloomington, Ill.*

De Garmo, Dr. Charles: Essentials of Method, *Boston*, 1889 ; Ethical Training in the Public Schools ; Am. Academy of Pol. and Soc. Science, publication No. 49, *Philadelphia ;* Language Work below the High Schools, *Bloomington, Ill.*, since 1887 ; The Herbartian System of Pedagogics, in the *Educational Review, New York*, vol. i., Nos. 1, 3, and 5 ; The Relation of Instruction to

Will Training, in the publications of the Am. Nat. Ed. Assoc., 1890 ; What does Apperception Mean ? in the *Public School Journal*, vol. x., No. 11, 1891, *Blooming- ton, Ill. ;* A popular View of Apperception, *Public School Journal*, vol. xii., No. 3, *Bloomington, Ill. ;* Coördination of Studies, *Educational Review*, vol. iv., No. 5 ; The Educational Value of Natural Science in Elementary Schools, in *Ed. Papers by Illinois Science Teachers*, i., 1889–90.

Donaldson : Lectures on the History of Education in Prussia and England, *Edinburgh*, 1874, mentions Ziller's work briefly and favorably.

Douglas, C. H. : Certain Views of Herbart on Mathematics and Natural Science, *Educational Review*, vol. iii., No. 5.

Findlay, J. J. : Herbartian Literature in English, *School and College*, October and November, 1892.

Hall, Dr. H. : Notes of the German Schools, contains refer- ences to Herbart.

Harris, Dr. W. T. : Apperception Defined, and Apperception *versus* Perception, in the *Public School Journal*, vol. xi., Nos. 2 and 5.

Herbart : The Science of Education, and The Æsthetic Revela- tion of the World, translated by Henry M. and Emmie Felkin — Swan Sonnenschein & Co., *London*, 1892.

Herbart : Psychology, translated by Miss M. K. Smith, Inter- national Education Series, *New York*, 1891.

Klemm, L. R. : European Schools, mentions the Herbartian Pedagogics, and gives some criticism, International Education Series, *New York*.

Lange : Ueber Apperception, translated by the Herbart Club in America, *Boston*, 1892.

Lindner : Empirical Psychology, translated by Dr. Charles De Garmo, *New York*, 1890.

Lukens, Dr. H. T. : Herbart's Psychological Basis of Teaching, Part II. of Th. B. Noss's Outlines of Psychology and Pedagogy, *Pittsburgh*, 1890.

McMurry, Dr. Charles A. : The Elements of General Method

based on the Principles of Herbart, *Bloomington, Ill.*, 1892 ; A Geography Plan for the Grades of the Common Schools, and Pioneer History Stories for the 3d and 4th Grade, *Bloomington, Ill.*, 1891 ; How to Conduct the Recitation, Teachers' Manuals, No. 13, *New York* and *Chicago*.

McMurry, Dr. Frank : The Moral Value of Fairy Tales and Imaginative Literature for Children, in *Public School Journal, Bloomington, Ill.*, vol. x., No. 11, and vol. xi., No. 3 ; Relation of Sciences to the other Studies, in *Ed. Papers by Illinois Science Teachers*, i., 1889-90, *Peoria, Ill.;* Value of Herbartian Pedagogy for Normal Schools, in *Proceedings of Nat. Ed. Assoc.* for 1892.

Prince, J. T. : Methods in German Schools, mentions the Herbartian Pedagogics briefly, and gives some criticism.

Ribot, T. : German Psychology of To-day, contains a digest of Herbart's psychology, *New York*, 1880.

Salmon, Lucy M. : The Teaching of History in the Elementary Schools, *Educational Review, New York*, vol. i., No. 5, contains brief reference to the principles of the historical stages of culture and concentration.

Smith, Margaret K. : Herbart's Life, three articles in the *New England Journal of Education*, 1889.

Ufer : Introduction to the Pedagogy of Herbart, translated by J. C. Zinser, edited by Charles De Garmo — D. C. Heath & Co.

Van Liew, C. C. : Life of Herbart and Development of his Pedagogical Doctrines — Swan Sonnenschein & Co., *London*, 1893.

Ward : Article in the *Encyclopædia Britannica*, on Herbart, important psychologically.

THE GREAT EDUCATORS.

NOTICES OF THE SERIES.

"Admirably conceived in a truly philosophic spirit and executed with unusual skill. It is rare to find books on pedagogy at once so instructive and so interesting. . . . I hope to read them all, which is more than I can say of any other series."—WILLIAM PRESTON JOHNSTON, *Tulane University.*

"The Scribners are rendering an important service to the cause of education in the production of the 'Great Educators Series.'"—*Journal of Education.*

"We have not too many series devoted to the history and the theory of education, and the one represented at the present moment by the two volumes before us promises to take an important place—a leading place—amongst the few we have."—*London Educational Times.*

ARISTOTLE.

The whole of ancient pedagogy is Professor Davidson's subject, the course of education being traced up to Aristotle,—an account of whose life and system forms, of course, the main portion of the book,—and down from that great teacher, as well as philosopher, through the decline of ancient civilization. An appendix discusses "The Seven Liberal Arts," and paves the way for the next work in chronological sequence,—Professor West's, on Alcuin. The close relations between Greek education and Greek social and political life are kept constantly in view by Professor Davidson. A special and very attractive feature of the work is the citation, chiefly in English translation, of passages from original sources expressing the spirit of the different theories described.

"I am very glad to see this excellent contribution to the history of education. Professor Davidson's work is admirable. His topic is one of the most profitable in the entire history of culture."—W. T. HARRIS, *U. S. Commissioner of Education.*

"'Aristotle' is delightful reading. I know nothing in English that covers the field of Greek Education so well. You will find it very hard to maintain this level in the later works of the series, but I can wish you nothing better than that you may do so."—G. STANLEY HALL, *Clark University.*

ALCUIN.

Professor West aims to develop the story of educational institutions in Europe from the beginning of the influence of Christianity on education to the origin of the Universities and the first beginnings of the modern movement. A careful analysis is made of the effects of Greek and Roman thought on the educational theory and practice of the early Christian, and their great system of schools, and its results are studied with care and in detail. The personality of Alcuin enters largely into the story, because of his dominating influence in the movement.

"Die von Ihnen mir freundlichst zugeschickte Schrift des Herrn Professor West über Alcuin habe ich mit lebhaftem Interesse gelesen und bin überrascht davon in Nord America eine so eingehende Beschäftigung mit unserer Vorzeit und eine so ausgebreitete Kenntniss der Literatur über diesen Gegenstand zu finden. Es sind mir wohl Einzelheiten begegnet an denen ich etwas auszusetzen fand, die ganze Auffassung und Darstellung aber kann ich nur als sehr wohl gelungen und zutreffend bezeichnen."—PROFESSOR WATTENBACH, *Berlin.*

"I take pleasure in saying that 'Alcuin' seems to me to combine careful, scholarly investigation with popularity, and condensation with interest or detail, in a truly admirable way."—Professor G. T. LADD, *of Yale.*

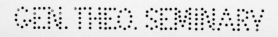
GEN. THEO. SEMINARY

ABELARD.

M. Compayré, the well-known French educationist, has prepared in this volume an account of the origin of the great European Universities that is at once the most scientific and the most interesting in the English language. Naturally the University of Paris is the central figure in the account; and the details of its early organization and influence are fully given. Its connection with the other great universities of the Middle Ages and with modern university movement is clearly pointed out. Abelard, whose system of teaching and disputation was one of the earliest signs of the rising universities, is the typical figure of the movement; and M. Compayré has given a sketch of his character and work, from an entirely new point of view, that is most instructive.

" ' Abelard ' may fairly be called the founder of university education in Europe, and we have in this volume a description of his work and a careful analysis of his character. As the founder of the great Paris University in the thirteenth century the importance of his work can hardly be overestimated. The chapter devoted to Abelard himself is an intensely interesting one, and the other chapters are of marked value, devoted as they are to the origin and early history of universities. . . . The volume is a notable educational work."— *Boston Daily Traveler.*

LOYOLA.

This work is a critical and authoritative statement of the educational principles and method adopted in the Society of Jesus, of which the author is a distinguished member. The first part is a sketch, biographical and historical, of the dominant and directing personality of Ignatius, the Founder of the order, and his comrades, and of the establishment and early administrations of the Society. In the second an elaborate analysis of the system of studies is given, beginning with an account of Aquaviva and the *Ratio Studiorum,* and considering, under the general heading of "the formation of the master," courses of literature and philosophy, of divinity and allied sciences, repetition, disputation, and dictation; and under that of "formation of the scholar," symmetry of the courses pursued, the prelection, classic literatures, school management and control, examinations and graduation, grades and courses.

" This volume on St. Ignatius of ' Loyola and the Educational System of the Jesuits,' by the Rev. Thomas Hughes, will probably be welcomed by others besides those specially interested in the theories and methods of education. Written by a member of the Jesuit Society, it comes to us with authority, and presents a complete and well-arranged survey of the work of educational development carried out by Ignatius and his followers."— *London Saturday Review.*

FROEBEL.

Friedrich Froebel stands for the movement known both in Europe and in this country as the New Education, more completely than any other single name. The kindergarten movement, and the whole development of modern methods of teaching, have been largely stimulated by, if not entirely based upon, his philosophical exposition of education. It is not believed that any other account of Froebel and his work is so complete and exhaustive, as the author has for many years been a student of Froebel's principles and methods not only in books, but also in actual practice in the kindergarten   Mr. Bowen is a frequent examiner of kin-

dergartens, of the children in them, and of students who are trained to be kindergarten teachers.

" No one, in England or America, is fitted to give a more sympathetic or lucid interpretation of Froebel than Mr. Courthope Bowen. . . . Mr. Bowen's book will be a most important addition to any library, and no student of Froebel can afford to do without it."—KATE DOUGLAS WIGGIN, *New York City.*

HERBART.

In this book, President De Garmo has given, for the first time in the English language, a systematic analysis of the Herbartian theory of education, which is now so much studied and discussed in Great Britain and the United States, as well as in Germany. Not only does the volume contain an exposition of the theory as expounded by Herbart himself, but it traces in detail the development of that theory and the additions to it made by such distinguished names as Ziller, Story, Frick, Rein, and the American School of Herbartians. Especially valuable will be found Dr. De Garmo's careful and systematic exposition of the problems that centre around the concentration and correlation of studies. These problems are generally acknowledged to be the most pressing and important at present before the teachers of the country.

" Some one has said there can be no great need without the means of supplying such need, and no sooner did the fraternity realize its need of a knowledge of the essentials of Herbart than Dr. De Garmo's excellent work on ' Herbart and the Herbartians,' by Scribner's Sons of New York, appeared, a book which, costing but a dollar, gives all that the teacher really needs, and gives it with devout loyalty and sensible discrimination. It is the work of a believer, a devotee, an enthusiast, but it is the masterpiece of the writer who has not forgotten what he owes to his reputation as a scholar in his devotion to his master."—*Journal of Education.*

THE ARNOLDS.

No book heretofore published concerning one or both of the Arnolds has accomplished the task performed in the present instance by Sir Joshua Fitch. A long-time colleague of Matthew Arnold in the British Educational Department, the author—leaving biography aside—has, with unusual skill, written a succinct and fascinating account of the important services rendered to the educational interests of Great Britain by the Master of Rugby and his famous son. The varied and successful efforts of the latter in behalf of a better secondary education during his long official career of thirty-five years as Inspector of Training Schools, no less than the notable effect produced at Rugby by the inspiring example of Thomas Arnold's high-minded character and enthusiastic scholarship, are admirably presented. Whatever in the teaching of both seems likely to prove of permanent value has been judiciously selected by the author from the mass of their writings, and incorporated in the present volume. The American educational public, which cannot fail to acknowledge a lasting debt of gratitude to the Arnolds, father and son, will certainly welcome this sympathetic exposition of their influence and opinions.

" The book is opportune, for the Arnoldian tradition, though widely diffused in America, is not well based on accurate knowledge and is pretty much in the air. Dr. Fitch seems the fittest person by reason of his spiritual sympathy with the father and his personal association with the son, to sketch in this brief way the two most typical modern English educators. And he has done his work almost ideally well within his limitations of purpose. . . . The two men live in these pages as they were."—*Educational Review,* New York.

The Great Educators

Edited by Nicholas Murray Butler

"Just in the right time to meet the needs of a large number of teachers who are casting about to find something fundamental and satisfying on the theory of education."—HON. W. T. HARRIS, *U. S. Commissioner of Education.*

HORACE MANN and Public Education in the United States. **By** B. A. HINSDALE, Ph.D., LL.D., Professor of the Art and Science of Teaching in the University of Michigan. 12mo. $1.00 net.

THOMAS and **MATTHEW ARNOLD** and their Influence on English Education. By SIR JOSHUA FITCH, LL.D., Late Inspector of Training Colleges in England. 12mo. $1.00 net.

ARISTOTLE and the Ancient Educational Ideals. By THOMAS DAVIDSON, M.A., LL.D. 12mo. $1.00 net.

ALCUIN and the Rise of the Christian Schools. By Professor ANDREW F. WEST, Ph.D., of the University of Princeton. 12mo. $1.00 net

ABELARD and the Origin and Early History of Universities. By JULES GABRIEL COMPAYRE, Rector of the University of Lyons, France. 12mo. $1.00 net.

LOYOLA and the Educational System of the Jesuits. By THOMAS HUGHES, S.J. 12mo. $1.00.

FROEBEL and Education through Self Activity. By H. COURTHOPE BOWEN, M.A., Late Lecturer on Education in the University of Cambridge. 12mo. $1.00 net.

HERBART and the Herbartians. By CHARLES DE GARMO, Ph.D., President of Swarthmore College. 12mo. $1.00 net.

ROUSSEAU and Education according to Nature. By THOMAS DAVIDSON, M.A., LL.D. 12mo. $1.00 net.

PESTALOZZI and the Modern Elementary School. By M. A. PINLOCHE, Professor in the University of Lille, France.

12mo. $1.00 net.

The history of great educators is, from an important point of view, the history of education. These volumes are not only biographies, but concise yet comprehensive accounts of the leading movement in educational thought, and furnish a genetic account of educational history. Ancient education, the rise of the Christian schools, the foundation and growth of universities, and the great modern movements suggested by the names, are adequately described and criticised.

Copies, subject to the privilege of return, will be sent for examination to any Teacher upon receipt of the Net Price.
The price paid for the sample copy will be returned, or a free copy inclosed, upon receipt of an order for TEN or more copies for Introduction.
Correspondence is invited, and will be cheerfully answered. Catalogue sent free.

CHARLES SCRIBNER'S SONS,

153-157 FIFTH AVE., NEW YORK.